VOL. 1

DRUMMING
IN ALL DIRECTIONS

A System for Achieving Creative Control

BY DAVID DIENI

Edited by: Charylu Roberts

Design and Layout: Charylu Roberts, O.Ruby Productions

Cover Design: Sheila Gunn

Photographs: Sam Huie

ISBN 978-1-4950-9969-4

DID PRODUCTIONS

EXCLUSIVELY DISTRIBUTED BY

HAL•LEONARD®

ACKNOWLEDGMENTS

Special thanks to Doreen Hoang, Carlos Almeida and Adam Grant.

ABOUT THE AUTHOR

David Dieni is a graduate of both the Oberlin Conservatory of Music and San Francisco Conservatory of Music. As a drummer and percussionist, his experience encompasses everything from rock to classical, jazz, and musicals.

During his time with the Sacramento Philharmonic, Stockton Symphony, Springfield (MA) Symphony and California Pops Orchestra, David has performed with Carol Channing, Dave Brubeck, Judy Collins, Sylvia McNair and Luciano Pavarotti.

He was in the West Coast revival of *Jacques Brel is Alive and Well and Living in Paris* at the Marin Theater Company; performed with Sharon McKnight in California Cabaret's production of *Ruthless!* and with Lee Meriwether in *Happy End.*

In 2011, Dom Famularo invited David to assist in creating the new, revised edition of George Stone's seminal *Accents and Rebounds.* The team of collaborators also included Danny Gottlieb and John Riley. The new edition was released on Alfred in 2012.

David has recorded for Koch International on the Ursula Le Guin/Eli Armer collaboration, *Uses of Music in Uttermost Parts*, and is a recipient of a Meet the Composer grant for his own music.

He maintains a busy teaching schedule at his SF Drum School, which has proved an active training ground for the next generation of drummers and percussionists.

David is a member of the Sabian Education Network and the D'Addario Education Collective (Promark, Evans).

FOREWORD

I have enjoyed meeting and teaching many dedicated students. I must say, Dave Dieni has proven to have an incredible passion to learn and push himself to new levels in percussion.

His first lesson he attended with his dad, Dominick. In the 1950s, Dom was a student in Boston with George Lawrence Stone, author of *Stick Control* and *Accents and Rebounds*. Such great stories he shared inspiring both Dave and I.

Dave, now living in San Francisco, continued to fly back east to New York to study with me for several years.

Dave analyzed each aspect of technique movement and has a very inquisitive way of searching out information and ideas about drumming. He challenges all his students and helps them to discover their own musical journey.

Dave performs many styles of percussion and drum set playing in different musical genres. It was his quest to seek out more options in drumming independence.

That leads to his current idea of *Drumming In All Directions: Achieving Freedom and Creative Control at the Kit*. He discovered a systematic approach to challenge your hands and feet with pushing the boundaries of creative expressive freedom.

This book is a portal for you to enter a path of options for a deeper understanding of drum set performance.

Enjoy the journey of experiencing *Drumming In All Directions!*

Dom Famularo
Drumming's Global Ambassador

TABLE OF CONTENTS

PREFACE

As a kid, household chores were a tough sell. But there was one big exception—my dad was a drummer. Bounding downstairs when he had a gig, I would haul his Rogers Holiday kit to the car and pack everything with immense accomplishment. I was a drummer on the make!

My dad grew up in Springfield, Massachusetts and like Joe Morello a few years earlier; he studied with the great George Stone. Every two weeks he rode a bus to Boston and made his way to the Stone Drum and Xylophone School on 61 Hanover Street. It was right next door to an old burlesque theater!

Under Stone, my dad worked through *Stick Control* and before it was published, *Accents and Rebounds*. He amassed a collection of exercises in Stone's own hand. Years later I would sift through those cryptic notes wondering what it all meant.

When I started drumming, my dad through his time with Stone, made me aware of good technique, precision, coordination, control, movement and balance. I was too young to understand, but I was joining the Stone lineage! My training took me through two conservatories and some amazing teachers but a feeling something was missing dogged me. I just didn't know what.

Rummaging through bins one day in a music store, I found *It's Your Move* by Dom Famularo. As I flipped through the pages it hit me: here it finally was! In his book, Dom revealed the connection between Stone, Moeller and Gladstone, the three masters of motion and natural drumming. Together they comprise the total spectrum of drum technique, which in turn is our heritage.

Soon after, a trip to Dom's studio was a necessary part of visiting family. Driving to Bridgeport and riding the ferry across the Sound to quaint Port Jefferson, I entered Dom's studio and began learning the techniques of natural motion. There were many late nights at a practice pad but my benchmark was always the joy of playing and complete freedom at the kit that all great drummers own.

It's been a long road from the boy mulling over Stone's penciled notes to performer and teacher, but a question has developed along the way: how do we achieve total freedom and control at our instrument?

I offer this book as one answer to that question. Understanding motion and balance as central to freedom and control, this book is itself a journey… to creative expression, to *Drumming In All Directions!*

I dedicate this book to:

Dominick Dieni—My dad and the drummer before me.

The teachers who guided me to a higher understanding of music, movement and balance: Warren Myers, Alan Dawson, Fred Hinger, Jack Van Geem and Dom Famularo.

My students, who have taught me so much.

And all you who will journey into the world of the masters of motion!

Drum Set Key

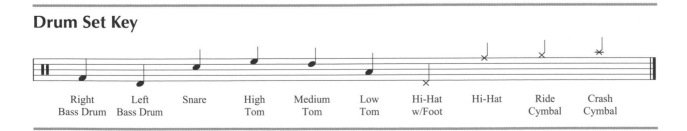

| Right Bass Drum | Left Bass Drum | Snare | High Tom | Medium Tom | Low Tom | Hi-Hat w/Foot | Hi-Hat | Ride Cymbal | Crash Cymbal |

COORDINATION BREAKDOWN

Crash and Burn

You're grooving hard and suddenly—BANG! A cool idea pops into your head. You even feel it in your body. Warp speed, limbs steal it and in a dance of awesome precision, throw it out into the world!

Or maybe this happens…

Your limbs tangle in an uncooperative mess and it all backfires. That idea—your little nugget of musical genius—crumbles like an old cookie.

What a feeling, huh?

You know it's about coordination, but what do you practice? Wrestling a vague coordination problem, we can forget our goal—creative freedom; even complete connection to the music! How do we practice that?

A good question! Let's first get straight with our terms…

What Is Coordination?

Drummers often use *coordination* and *independence* interchangeably. They're not the same! When interdependence is added to the mix, the descriptions often dissolve into poetic abstractions. This helps nobody. Let's look at these three concepts and find practical, drummer-based definitions.

A good general description of coordination is the ability to use our four limbs in a relaxed and efficient way regardless of any groove or pattern. Coordination breaks down into 3 basic levels, each concerned with greater degrees of control:

Level 1: *Control of individual limbs* and integration of like limbs.

We first learn control of each limb, without connection to the others.

We usually start with hands playing solo, then work on integrating them into a single functioning unit. Next, we follow the same path with the feet—individual control and then integration into a cohesive unit.

Level 2: *Independence* – control of two or more limbs playing together.

Independence is control beyond the integrating of like limbs. The spectrum runs from any limb combination playing the same rhythms to any limb combination playing different rhythms.

Traditionally, drummers work on Independence by playing one pattern against another until the combined result is dialed into our muscle memory. We might assign any limb combination to these patterns. Once pattern A can be played against pattern B, we've achieved independence. But only with those 2 patterns! Now we must practice pattern A with pattern C and so on. Eventually we might have 20 or 30 different pattern combinations at our disposal to express ourselves in whatever style of music we play.

Maybe you see the limits of independence? We want connection to the music. We strive for unhampered creative control so we can follow the music through its every ebb and flow. That's really the definition of complete expression. How can we do that with 20 or 30 coordination patterns? There must be something beyond independence!

Level 3: *Interdependence* – control of any limb combination pattern moving fluidly to any other limb combination pattern. All limbs are working together, completely at the service of musical expression!

Independence and interdependence are similar, but different types of limb control:

Independence is about *fragmentation*: We approach music by figuring what limbs play which composite rhythms and how to piece it all together.

Interdependence is about *integration*. We approach music with the complete picture in mind. The limbs understand how to work together and create the whole. It's the final development of coordination!

OK, so you're grooving hard and suddenly…BANG! With independence, your limbs work as separate units piecing together the whole of your idea. With interdependence, your limbs are an integrated unit. They understand how to work together to realize your idea.

I don't know about you, but integration is where I want to go! So how do we get there?

From Motion-Balance to Creative Freedom

There's a natural progression of single limb coordination and like limb integration through independence to interdependence. That progression is based on control. Control is the beginning of our journey to creative freedom!

This brings me back to: What is coordination? If coordination is control, than what kind of control are we talking about?

Control is a combination of *Motion* and *Balance*.

Motion refers to the natural motion techniques of George Stone and Sanford Moeller. Free stroke and Moeller technique are about making relaxed throwing motions and using the rebound energy of the stick or beater.

Balance is our ability to remain in a position or move to other positions while retaining relaxed control.

We now have a more nuanced definition of coordination:

> *Successful coordination occurs when techniques of natural motion incorporate proper balance of the body at the kit and an overall relaxed approach.*

There's a dance-like relationship between motion and balance, each affecting the other within an ever-changing musical fabric. I call this symbiotic relationship *Motion-Balance*. It's the foundation of coordination!

Without motion-balance, coordination is hampered and is more like a math problem. The furthest we can go is a compromised independence—figuring how one pattern fits into another, how one limb plays against another. We likely encounter familiar problems of groove, feel and time. Or put another way—problems of creative expression!

With motion-balance, coordination transforms into a dance between all limbs, a dance beyond independence to interdependence.

Perhaps you now see a shortcoming in the hands first, feet second approach to learning drums? We often view the hands and feet as separate animals with different techniques. In order to achieve motion-balance, we must use the same techniques of natural motion and balance for all limbs!

Enter Drumming In All Directions

DID abandons the usual fragmented approach of traditional independence studies. By starting with motion-balance, it embraces integration at the outset!

Instead of coordinating pattern combinations, *DID* starts with coordinating limb-motions. There are 50 limb-motion combinations, 50 ways that all 4 limbs combine into alternating motions. These are progressively ordered in the *Limb Matrix* and include 2-limb motions, unison pairings; 3-limb and 4-limb motions.

The motions are brought to life, challenged and developed by a series of *Control Workouts*. Each workout takes a specific figure I call a *Rhythm-Melody* and carries it through 15 exercise variations. The rhythm-melodies are figures elemental to all music!

By combining the limb motions in anything you might play with patterns fundamental to any music you might play, *Drumming In All Directions* will transform your playing by developing motion-balance.

You'll apply what you've learned in a more creative setting with *Groove Melodies* based on the control workouts. Finally, you'll push your control even further by adding timekeeping ostinatos and ride patterns to the limb motions.

Using this fundamental motion-balance approach, you'll develop the proper muscle memory and playing experience to build a solid coordination technique. If your drumming reflexes are tuned to these basic limb motions, music is easier to play because all music has these motions!

As you develop motion-balance, playing becomes effortless and fun. You'll feel the groove from brain to body. You'll achieve a new freedom of expression that's like flying by the seat of your pants—You'll be drumming in all directions!

Questions? Comments? Contact me at *www.daviddieni.com*

GENERAL PRINCIPLES

Motion-Balance requires an understanding of how the body works when drumming. Essential are techniques allowing natural movement and a relaxed, ergonomic approach.

We always want to achieve maximum results with minimal effort. Never forget that! Let's first consider natural motion techniques.

PRINCIPLES OF MOTION

Techniques of Natural Drumming

Free stroke and Moeller technique represent a historic body of drumming knowledge and a deeply fulfilling area of study. Let's get started by examining the basic working principles!

Natural drumming techniques make use of the body as it actually functions to execute relaxed, fluid and continuous stroke motions.

The arms and legs are a system of drumming hinges that correspond to our joints. For the arm, these include the fingers, wrist, forearm, elbow and shoulder. For the leg, these include the ankle, knee and hip. Each drumming hinge must remain relaxed into the next going all the way up the arm and leg. It's especially important the shoulder doesn't grip the arm. Let the arm hang loose. The same is true for the leg connecting to the hip.

The most important natural drumming techniques are free stroke and Moeller. The whipping motions of Moeller technique are only possible once the free stroke is mastered. Because of this, free stroke technique is fundamental and our starting point for developing motion-balance.

The Free Stroke

In making a free stroke, the stick is thrown into the head and allowed to do what it wants—rebound off without the hand or arm interfering! The hand simply rides the stick back up for the next stroke, the arm allowing a relaxed follow through. This is called accepting the rebound. The same holds true for the foot—it throws the beater into the bass drum head and rides the pedal back as the beater rebounds. The leg provides a relaxed follow through.

Think of the free stroke as throwing and catching the stick, not pushing and pulling. We relax our hand and arm muscles after throwing the stick just like after throwing a ball. It's easy with a ball because it leaves our hand after the throw, but the stick tip is always connected to our hand by the shaft. This makes it possible to never turn off our muscles. Instead of releasing the ball (stick tip) and catching it on the rebound, we push the stick into the head, choke off the rebound and then pull the stick off the head. The stick is always faster than you. Let it rebound!

It's important to stay relaxed from throw to rebound so there is a follow through up along all the drum hinges. For the arms, this means the stick rebound energy travels freely up the arm to the shoulder. For the leg, beater rebound energy travels freely up to the hip. By not choking off the rebound and allowing a follow through along the hinges, tension is avoided and rebound energy can be redirected into making the next stroke or series of strokes.

Stroke Types

There are two types of free strokes: *primary* and *control strokes*. In a primary stroke, a stick thrown from a given height rebounds back to that height. The full stroke is a special example of a primary stroke. A stick thrown from high position (stick pointing straight up) rebounds back to high position. Taps are primary strokes made close to the head and are essentially stick dribbles.

Control strokes are about positioning the stick at any height you need. There are two types of control strokes: *downstrokes* and *upstrokes*.

In a downstroke, a stick thrown from a high position rebounds to a lower position. The hand and arm absorb the stick rebound energy. In an upstroke, the stick plays a lower position stroke and rises to a higher position. In this instance, the hand and arm assist in the stick lift.

Our drumming vocabulary regardless of style is made up of these four strokes: full strokes, taps, upstrokes and downstrokes. Everything you could ever play is defined by these four strokes! They comprise the fundamental language of drumming. The four strokes allow us to make full use of stick and beater rebound; they allow us to make music!

The following control workouts and groove melodies are to be played first with free stroke technique. Only after free stroke mastery should you progress to the whipping stroke of Moeller technique and the accents it makes possible.

A qualified teacher is a great asset in learning natural drumming techniques. At the end of the chapter you'll find a list of educational materials for further study.

PRINCIPLES OF BALANCE

Proper balance is fundamental to relaxed control at the kit. Let's consider balance from three perspectives: bass drum technique, the drum throne, and finally overall posture.

The Bass Drum

The first time through the workouts, play the bass drum with feet *heels down*. Heels down helps with overall foot control by developing the shin and ankle muscles.

When playing *heels up*, rest position is actually feet on the pedals. The heels lift when strokes are made and return to the pedal after stroke completion. The result is like the feet are dancing on a cushion or air. Whether playing heels up or down, the foot makes contact with the pedal on the balls of the feet.

Spring tension on the pedal is obviously a personal thing. Given that, keep the spring loose. A looser spring allows your foot to feel the natural rebound of the beater off the drumhead. It trains the foot to make strong, relaxed and fluid strokes. A too tight spring interferes with natural rebound and foot sensitivity. A great exercise is to practice pedal strokes with the spring disconnected. The foot will learn to make quick, relaxed free strokes, or else the beater will stick to the head!

The Drum Throne

The height of the throne should place the drummer at a comfortable sitting position. The thighs should be angled slightly down from hip to knee. If the thighs are angled down too much, the lower back is strained and the body will be off balance.

For proper sitting distance at the kit, the angle between the thigh and lower leg at the knee should be a bit more than 90 degrees. This can be achieved by positioning the ankles directly under the knees. If you sit too far from the kit, the ankles will be in a weak position.

Body Posture

Good posture and a strong core are essential to drumming.

Sit upright—no slouching, leaning backwards, forwards or off to a side. Sit more in the middle of the throne, not at the back or front edge of the seat. Sitting upright with good posture allows the lower back and abdominal muscles to relax. This in turn provides maximum freedom moving around the drums.

A common posture problem is using one or both feet as a prop for balance. This interferes with sensitivity and control. It also affects a drummer's time—especially when changing grooves or playing fills. Make sure both feet rest lightly on the pedals. Support the weight of both legs from your core and hips. Don't push your body weight down through your feet to the pedals!

FURTHER STUDY OF NATURAL DRUMMING TECHNIQUES

Books

1. *It's Your Move* by Dom Famularo with Joe Bergamini (Alfred Publishing Co.)

2. *Pedal Control* by Dom Famularo and Joe Bergamini (Alfred Publishing Co.)

DVDs

1. Joe Morello: *Drum Method 1: The Natural Approach to Technique*

2. Joe Morello and Danny Gottlieb: *Natural Drumming; Lessons 1 and 2, Lessons 3 and 4, Lessons 5 and 6* (Melbay)

3. Jim Chapin: *Speed, Power, Control, Endurance* (Alfred Publishing Co.)

4. Jojo Mayer: *Secret Weapons for the Modern Drummer* (Hudson Music)

5. Jojo Mayer: *Secret Weapons for the Modern Drummer, Part II* (Hudson Music)

HOW TO USE THIS BOOK

The Control Workouts

The exercises are organized in routines called *Control Workouts*. These in turn are divided in two parts: control workouts in duple time and control workouts in triplet time.

Both parts contain four workout groups. The routines in each group are based on a unique rhythm-melody carried through a 15-exercise variation grid.

The two-bar exercises comprising each routine are notated on a one-line staff. Lead limb/s play notes above the line; secondary limb/s play notes below the line. Limbs trade places at the end of each bar: secondary limbs become lead limbs. This ensures equal limb development!

The Limb Matrix

The limb matrix is a progressive ordering of all possible limb motions. It's our key to practicing the control workouts and achieving motion-balance.

There are 3 versions of the matrix, each one focusing on a specific area of coordination: 4-limb motions, 3-limb motions with a 1-limb ostinato, 2-limb motions with 2-limb ostinatos.

Depending on the matrix version, limbs are notated as follows: hands are R, L and H. The feet are r, l and f. This will be discussed in greater detail in the following Limb Matrix chapter.

Arrows are used to depict limb motions. Lead Limbs are left of the arrow, secondary limbs right of the arrow. *Lead limbs* initiate the motion and *secondary limbs* follow.

The following 2-limb motion is right hand to left hand alternating:

$$R \longrightarrow L$$

Limb Unisons are shown with multiple letters. The following 3-limb motion is right hand alternating with left hand-right foot unison:

$$R \longrightarrow Lr$$

Putting It All Together

Control workouts are performed with the motion variations of the Limb-Matrix.

Consider 2-limb motion 1A from the 4-Limb Matrix: **R ➞ L**

Let's use this motion to play exercise 10 from Duple Time Control Workout 1.1:

Example 1

If lead right hand plays notes above the staff line and secondary left hand plays notes below, the simplest way to play the exercise is both hands on snare drum. In the second bar, the pattern switches to a left hand lead.

Example 2

R L R L R L   R L R L R L R   L R L R L R   L R L R L R L

With both hands on snare, play all of Workout 1.1 slowly, without stopping. Repeat each line at least 4 to 8 times.

As you progress through the exercises, continuous variation and lead limb flipping will present challenges. You'll find the coordination of limb motions falling apart and limbs losing their place from bar to bar. This is a good thing! Slow, patient practice with much repetition of the exercises will condition the muscles and build the proper pathway between brain and limbs.

A general principle for approaching the material:

>*Learn the control workouts with the basic limb voicing of hands on the same instrument or hands stationary but on different instruments.*

Other voicing possibilities are presented in the chapter, *Guide to Limb Voicings*.

The Groove Melodies

Each group of control workouts is followed by a series of two-bar groove melodies. The melodies are a chance to apply motion-balance in a more creative setting.

The groove melodies appear in two forms: the "a" form notates the groove on a one-line staff just like the control workout exercises. This form can be used with any of the matrix limb combinations.

The "b" form voices the groove in standard drum set notation on a 5-line staff. This form transforms the groove into a melody between snare, toms and bass.

Both forms of the groove melodies leave out cymbal ride patterns and hi-hat foot patterns for ease of reading and ease of using different ostinatos.

THE 4-LIMB MATRIX

The 4-limb matrix contains 50 limb combinations, abbreviated as follows:

R = Right Hand   L = Left Hand

r = Right Foot   l = Left Foot

The limb combinations are divided into 4 groups: *2-limb motions, unison pairings, 3-limb motions* and *4-limb motions*.

There are 3 coordination levels within the 2-limb motions, unison pairings and 3-limb motions:

Level 1: Side-to-side alternating of same limbs. Right hand to left hand, right foot to left foot. This is the most natural of the three limb motions.

Level 2: Upper to lower body alternating between limbs on same side of body. Right hand to right foot, left hand to left foot. This is a less natural motion.

Level 3: A crisscross motion from upper to lower body. Right hand to left foot, left hand to right foot. This is the least natural of the three motions.

4-limb motions are an exception to the above. The resultant feel is more like level 2- up and down alternating.

The following examples are from the 4 groups of the 4-Limb Matrix:

- 2-Limb Motion, Level 1: **r ⟶ l**
  Right Foot alternates with Left Foot

- Unison Pairing, Level 2: **Ll ⟶ Rr**
  Left Hand – Left Foot Unison alternates with Right Hand – Right Foot Unison

- 3-Limb Motion, Level 3: **R ⟶ Lr**
  Right Hand alternates with Left Hand – Right Foot Unison

- 4-Limb Motion, Level 2: **L ⟶ Rrl**
  Left Hand alternates with Right Hand – Right Foot – Left Foot Unison

VARIATIONS IN 4-LIMB MOTION

2-Limb Motions

Level 1: Side-to-Side Alternating

    1. **R → L**   2. **L → R**

    3. **r → l**   4. **l → r**

Level 2: Up and Down Alternating

    5. **R → r**   6. **r → R**

    7. **L → l**   8. **l → L**

Level 3: Crosswise Alternating

    9. **R → l**   10. **l → R**

    11. **L → r**   12. **r → L**

Unison-Pairing Limb Motions

Level 1: Side-to-Side Alternating

    13. **R L → r l**   14. **r l → R L**

Level 2: Up and Down Alternating

    15. **R r → L l**   16. **L l → R r**

Level 3: Crosswise Alternating

    17. **R l → L r**   18. **L r → R l**

3-Limb Motions

Level 1: Side-to-Side Alternating

19. **R L ➝ r**   20. **r ➝ R L**

21. **R L ➝ l**   22. **l ➝ R L**

23. **r l ➝ R**   24. **R ➝ r l**

25. **r l ➝ L**   26. **L ➝ r l**

Level 2: Up and Down Alternating

27. **R r ➝ L**   28. **L ➝ R r**

29. **R r ➝ l**   30. **l ➝ R r**

31. **L l ➝ R**   32. **R ➝ L l**

33. **L l ➝ r**   34. **r ➝ L l**

Level 3: Crosswise Alternating

35. **R l ➝ L**   36. **L ➝ R l**

37. **R l ➝ r**   38. **r ➝ R l**

39. **L r ➝ R**   40. **R ➝ L r**

41. **L r ➝ l**   42. **l ➝ L r**

4 Limb Motions

Level 2: Up and Down Alternating

43. **R L r ➝ l**   44. **l ➝ R L r**

45. **R L l ➝ r**   46. **r ➝ R L l**

47. **R r l ➝ L**   48. **L ➝ R r l**

49. **L r l ➝ R**   50. **R ➝ L r l**

THE 3-LIMB MATRIX

The 3-limb matrix contains 2-limb motions and 3-limb motions, while the 4th limb plays an ostinato or time-keeping pattern.

The following 7 time-keeping/ostinato patterns are fundamental and will serve as our starting point:

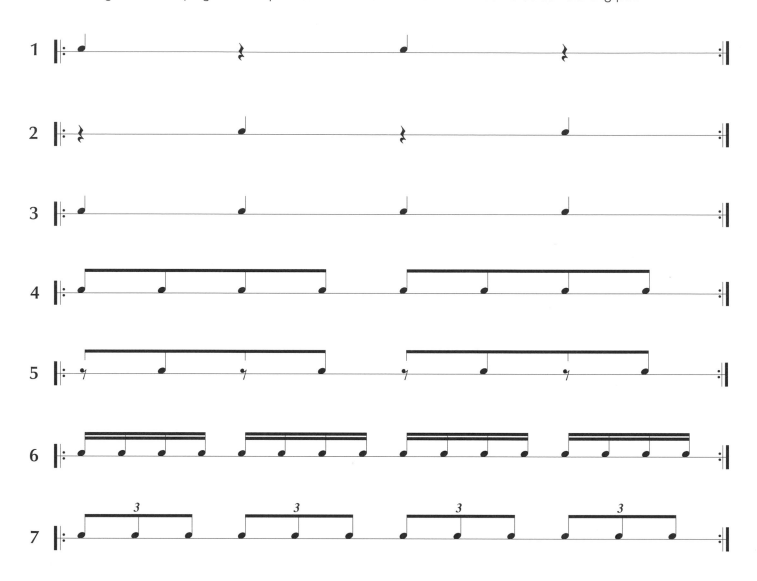

If the ostinato limb is a hand and the remaining limbs play the motion variations, the limb abbreviations are:

                H = Hand   r = right foot   l = left foot

If the ostinato limb is a foot, the control workout limbs are:

                R = Right Hand   L = Left Hand   f = foot

VARIATIONS IN 3-LIMB MOTION; 1-LIMB OSTINATO

2-Limb Motions

4th-Limb Ostinato – Hand

1. **H ⟶ r**   2. **r ⟶ H**

3. **H ⟶ l**   4. **l ⟶ H**

5. **r ⟶ l**   6. **l ⟶ r**

4th-Limb Ostinato – Foot

1. **R ⟶ L**   2. **L ⟶ R**

3. **R ⟶ f**   4. **f ⟶ R**

5. **L ⟶ f**   6. **f ⟶ L**

3-Limb Motions

4th-Limb Ostinato – Hand

1. **H r ⟶ l**   2. **l ⟶ H r**

3. **H l ⟶ r**   4. **r ⟶ H l**

5. **r l ⟶ H**   6. **H ⟶ r l**

4th-Limb Ostinato – Foot

1. **R L ⟶ f**   2. **f ⟶ R L**

3. **R f ⟶ L**   4. **L ⟶ R f**

5. **L f ⟶ R**   6. **R ⟶ L f**

THE 2-LIMB MATRIX

Variations in 2-Limb Motion; 2-Limbs Ostinato

When two limbs play ostinato or time keeping patterns, the remaining two limbs play the motion variations. This makes for a very short matrix!

Limb 1 → Limb 2   Limb 2 → Limb 1

However, there are three ways the 2-limb variations can be combined that pretty much cover all the ways we keep time at the kit:

I.   *Both hands play the motion variations; the feet play ostinatos:*

    1.   **R → L**   2.   **L → R**

This variation focuses on hand coordination. A common voicing is both hands on snare drum; feet play ostinatos on bass drum and hi-hat.

II. *Both feet play the motion variations; the hands play ostinatos:*

    1.   **r → l**   2.   **l → r**

This variation focuses on foot coordination. A common voicing is feet on double pedal. Hand ostinatos are cymbal ride and snare backbeat.

III. *Hand and foot play the motion variations; other hand and foot play ostinatos:*

    1.   **H → f**   2.   **f → H**

Most drum set playing falls in this category- comping patterns between snare and bass while playing a ride pattern with one hand and a secondary time keeping pattern with foot on hi-hat.

GUIDE TO LIMB VOICINGS

Voicing the Hands

There are four broad categories of how the hands can be voiced across the kit:

1. Both hands on the same instrument or each hand on a different instrument. No moving or traveling across the kit.

2. Both hands move together from instrument to instrument across the kit.

3   One hand remains on an instrument as the other hand travels across the kit.

4. Both hands travel freely of each other across the kit.

Example 2 (How To Use This Book) shows both hands stationary on the snare drum.

Example 3 shows hands on snare for only the 16th notes. On the 8th notes they travel to different drums—left hand on high tom, right hand on low tom.

Example 3

R   L R L R L   R L R L R L R   L   R L R L R L R L R L

For more complexity, the right hand can move between low and medium tom on 8th notes:

Example 4

R   L R L R L   R L R L R L R   L   R L R L R L R L R L

R   L R L R L   R L R L R L R   L   R L R L R L R L R L

The left hand can also move between high and medium tom on 8th notes:

Example 5

R   L R L R L   R L R L R L R   L   R L R L R L R L R L

R   L R L R L   R L R L R L R   L   R L R L R   L R L R L R L

Notice how the above voicings extend the exercise from two to four bars.

In Example 6, both hands play cymbals on 8th notes. 16th notes are split between snare and 3 toms with a clockwise motion, always starting on snare.

Example 6

R L R L R L   R L R L R L R   L   R L R L R   L R L R L R L

Let's change the above voicing by alternating streams of 16 notes from snare-high tom-low tom to snare-medium tom-low tom.

Example 7

R L R L R L   R L R L R L R   L   R L R L R   L R L R L R L

Example 8 retains cymbals on 8th notes. The drums are in a more broken pattern, starting with toms and moving to both hands on snare. LH plays high tom only; RH plays low tom only.

Example 8

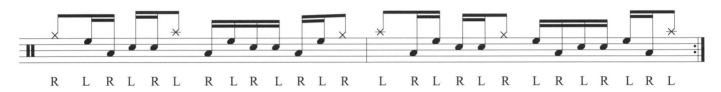

R L R L R L   R L R L R L R   L   R L R L R   L R L R L R L

Example 9 adds more complexity: medium tom plays when the 16th-note streams are long enough to include another tom after the high tom.

Example 9

R L R L R L   R L R L R L R   L   R L R L R   L R L R L R L

Examples 8 and 9 use broken patterns where each hand plays a specific tom. Another option is to maintain the melodic shape of the pattern. This means the hands cross each other as they travel across the kit.

Example 10

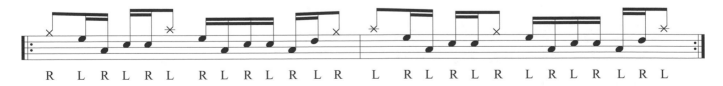

R L R L R L   R L R L R L R   L   R L R L R   L R L R L R L

These are just a few of the many ways the hands can be voiced across the kit. The feet are much simpler!

Voicing the Feet

The most common way to voice the feet is right foot on bass drum, left foot on hi-hat. Another is both feet on double pedal. I recommend using a double pedal for the control workouts, as there is no better way to promote limb equality. When more comfortable, your left foot will have the option of switching from double pedal to hi-hat during the workouts.

Two Important Points:

- Limb voicings are played through an entire workout, not just one exercise! The constant variation of the workouts means the voicing changes across the 15 exercises. You'll have the challenge of navigating these changes while maintaining the voicing.

- When the control workouts are played with ostinatos, the principles of hand voicing remain the same.

Let's consider voicing examples from each matrix. All examples involve the feet.

Voicing Examples: 4-Limb Matrix

Unison Pairing, Level 2: **L l ➞ R r**

Ex. 13 • Workout 2.2 – Part II

L – snare; R – ride cymbal; l – hi-hat; r – bass drum

L – snare; R – low to high tom; l & r – double pedal bass drum

L – snare to high tom; R – low to medium tom; l & r – double pedal bass drum

4-Limb Motion, Level 2: L → R r l

Ex. 6 • Workout 4.9 – Part II

2a

The following examples all have l – hi-hat and r – bass drum.

L – snare; R – ride cymbal

2b

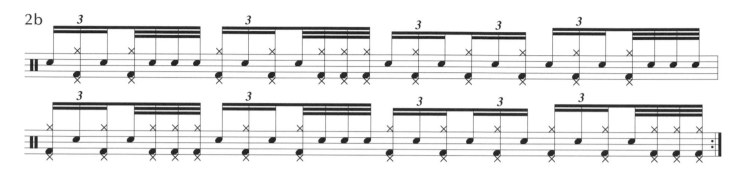

L – snare to clockwise around drums; R – snare

2c

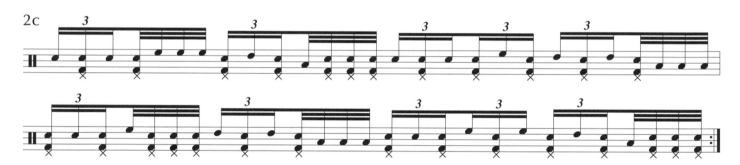

L & R – snare to crosswise around drums

2d

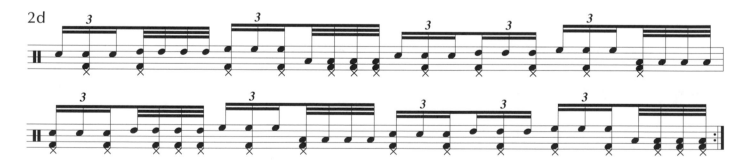

Voicing Examples: 3-Limb Matrix

3-Limb Motion: **R ⟶ L f**

Ex. 8 • Workout 4.6 – Part I

3a
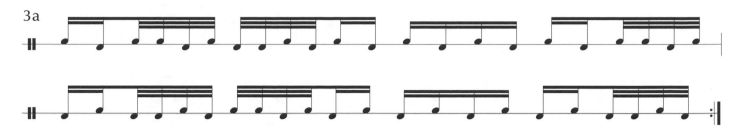

The following examples all have left foot ostinato on hi-hat; right foot on bass drum.

R – snare; L – ride cymbal

3b
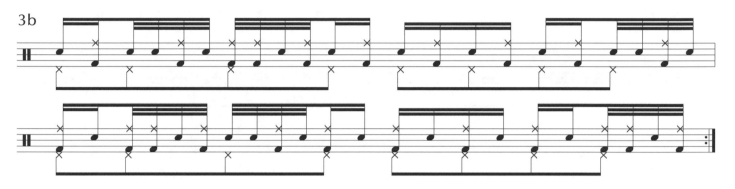

R – snare; L – snare to clockwise around drums

3c

R & L – snare to counterclockwise around drums

3d

Voicing Examples: 2-Limb Matrix

2 limbs play motion variations; 2 limbs play ostinatos

Ex. 15 • Workout 4.5 – Part II

4a

r ⟶ l: *Double pedal – bass drum*
Ostinatos: *L – hi-hat; R – snare*

4b

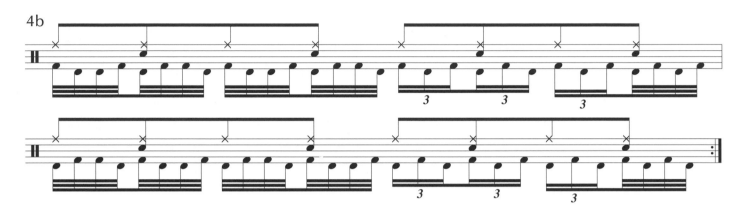

H ⟶ f: *L – snare; r – bass drum*
Ostinatos:: *l – hi-hat; R – ride cymbal*

4c

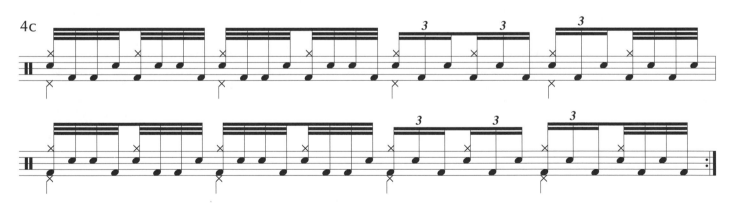

The above examples are just a few of the many available voicings. Remember, the voicings are not just applied to a single static exercise, but a dynamic 15-exercise workout involving constant variation.

The power of the Limb Matrix is that we don't have to read complicated music notation as in the above examples. We simply apply the selected limb motions to the workouts and focus all our attention on motion-balance. The only limit is our imagination!

PRACTICE GUIDE

General Considerations:

Practice the material in Part I before Part II. The Duple-Time Workouts will give you the facility to tackle the more challenging Triplet Time Workouts.

Start with the limb motions of the 4-Limb Matrix in the order presented. Mastering 2-limb motions provides a foundation for all that follows.

Use the simplest limb voicing- both hands on snare or each hand on a different sound source. In both cases the hands don't travel.

Play the control workouts with heels down to build greater foot control.

Repeat each exercise line at least 4 to 8 times! You can also play the exercises for a set time. For instance, 1 minute per line yields a 15-minute workout.

Practice Tips:

At first, play the workouts slowly without a metronome. Focus on the feeling of the limbs moving individually and together.

At the end of every bar, it's easy to lose track of which limb is lead and which is secondary. This fades away with patience and slow repetition!

It's difficult to play limb unisons without flams. Don't force unisons—stay relaxed! Accept flams as part of the journey. Use your ears and with repetition centering on relaxed, slow practice, the flams will merge into unisons.

Perform the routine exercises nonstop with relaxed, controlled playing at a consistent tempo. Speed is not important! It comes with an approach based on relaxed control and lots of repetition.

Most important of all—always keep in mind Motion and Balance! Motion is about playing with natural stick or beater rebound. Balance is about holding a position at the kit or moving between positions while maintaining relaxed control. Together motion and balance become motion-balance, an ever-changing dance of limb motions—the first step on the coordination road to interdependence and creative freedom!

PART I

Motion-Balance
in Duple Time

Control Workouts and Groove Melodies
Groups 1–4

Duple Time 1.1

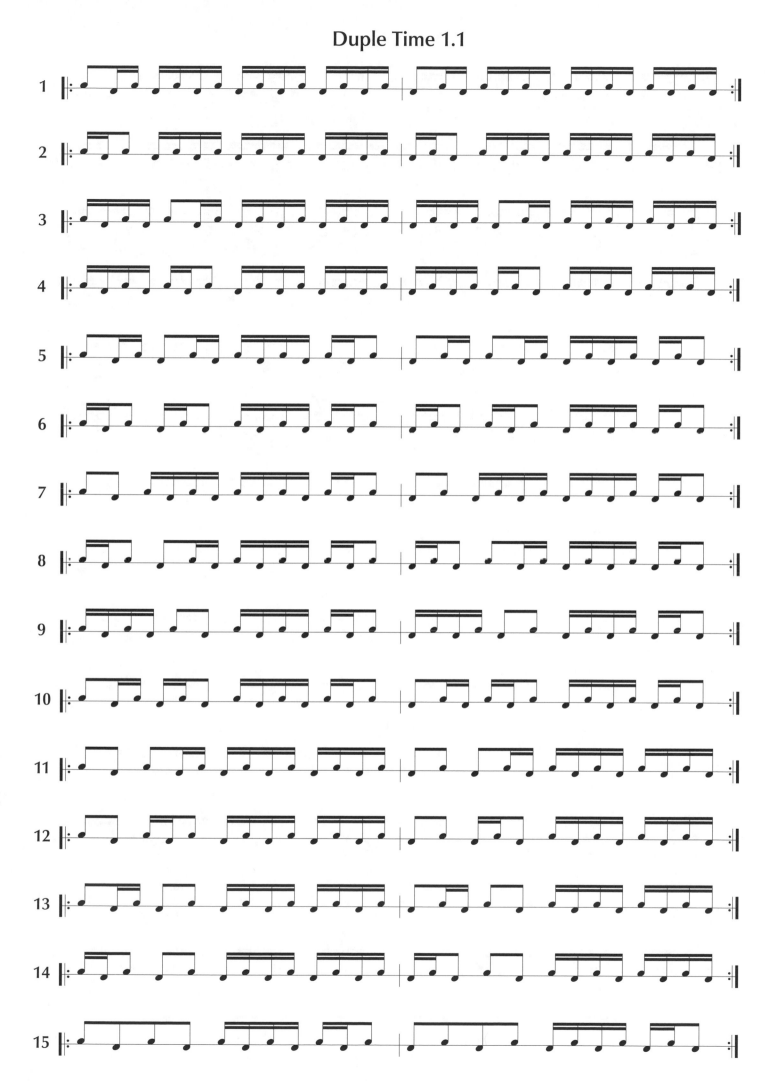

Duple Time 1.2

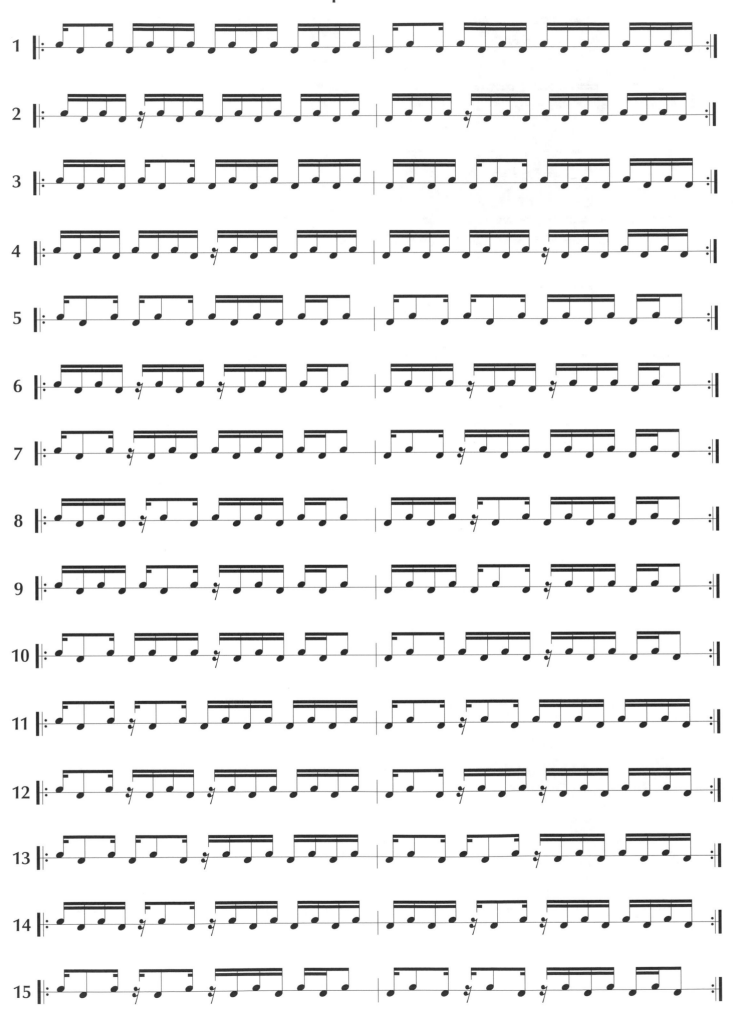

Groove Melodies 1

Groove Melodies 1

Duple Time 2.1

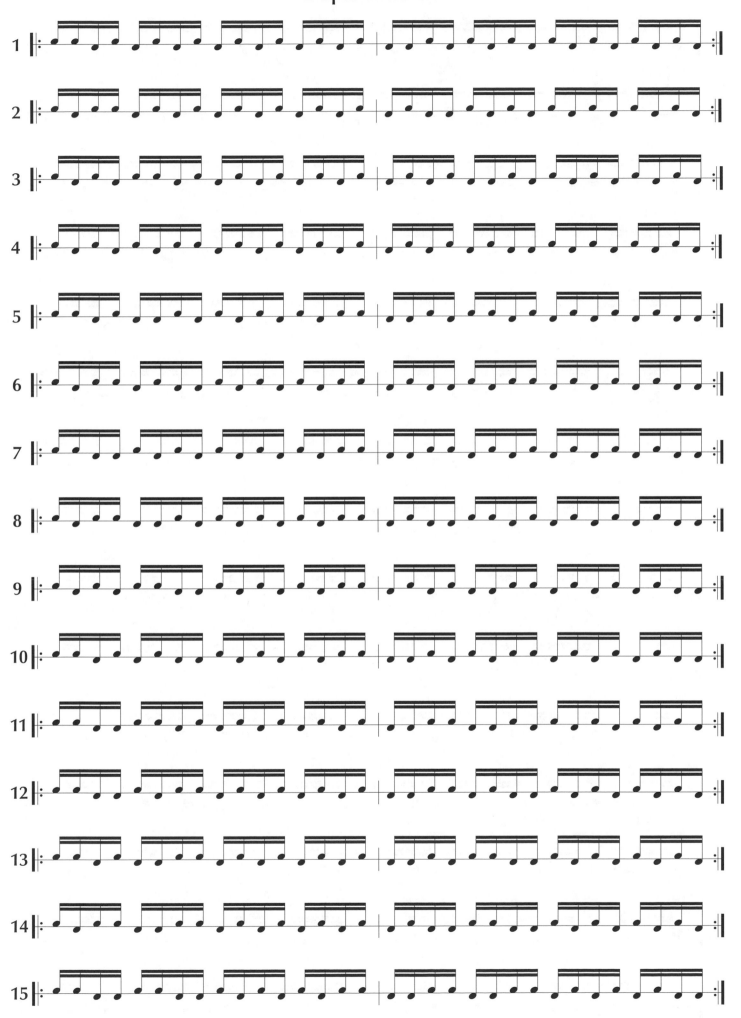

Duple Time 2.2

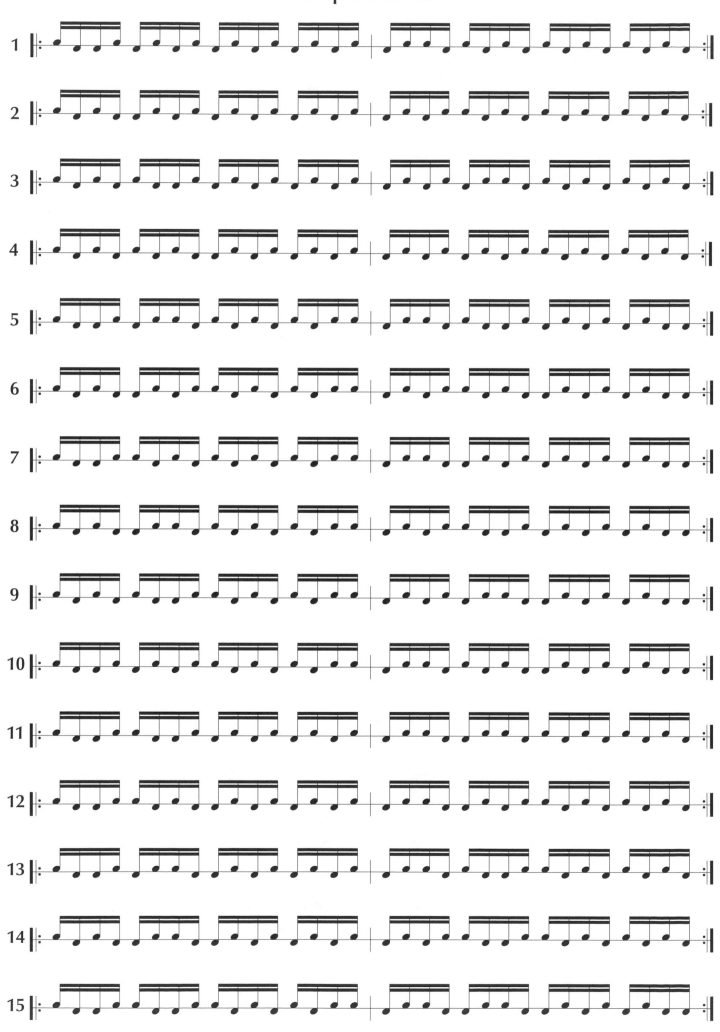

Groove Melodies 2

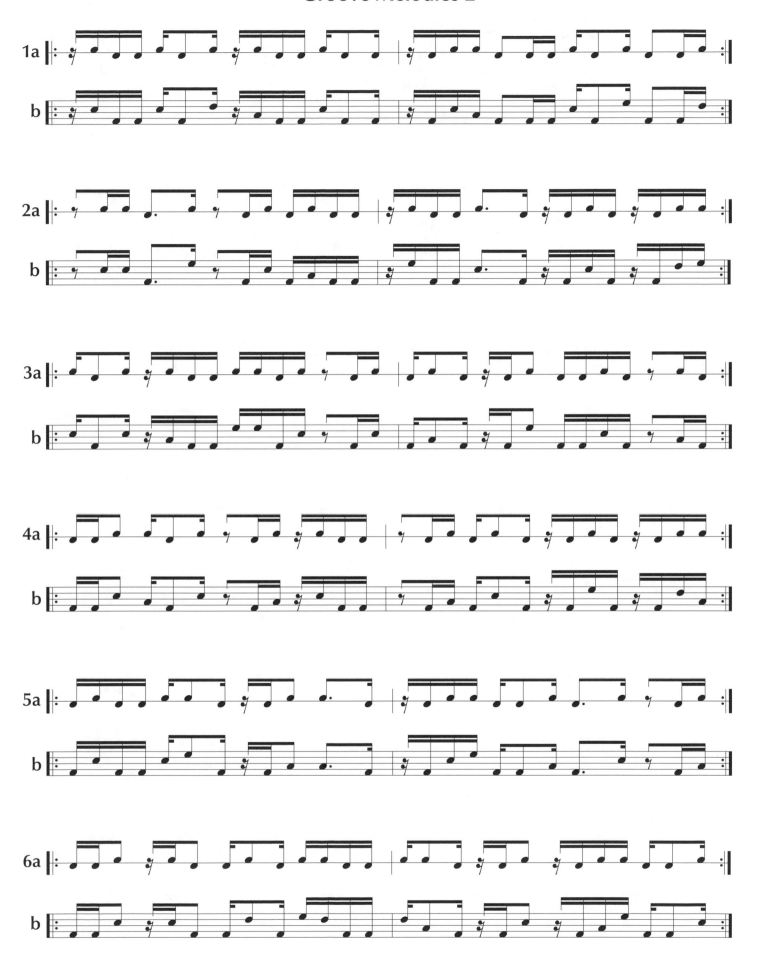

Groove Melodies 2

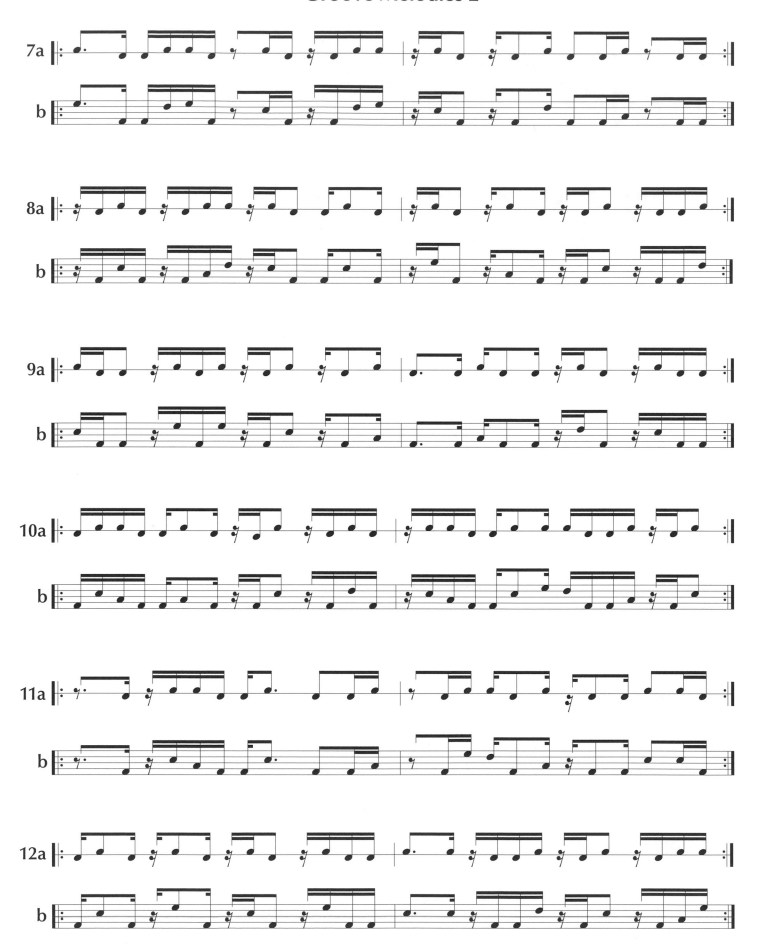

Duple Time 3.1

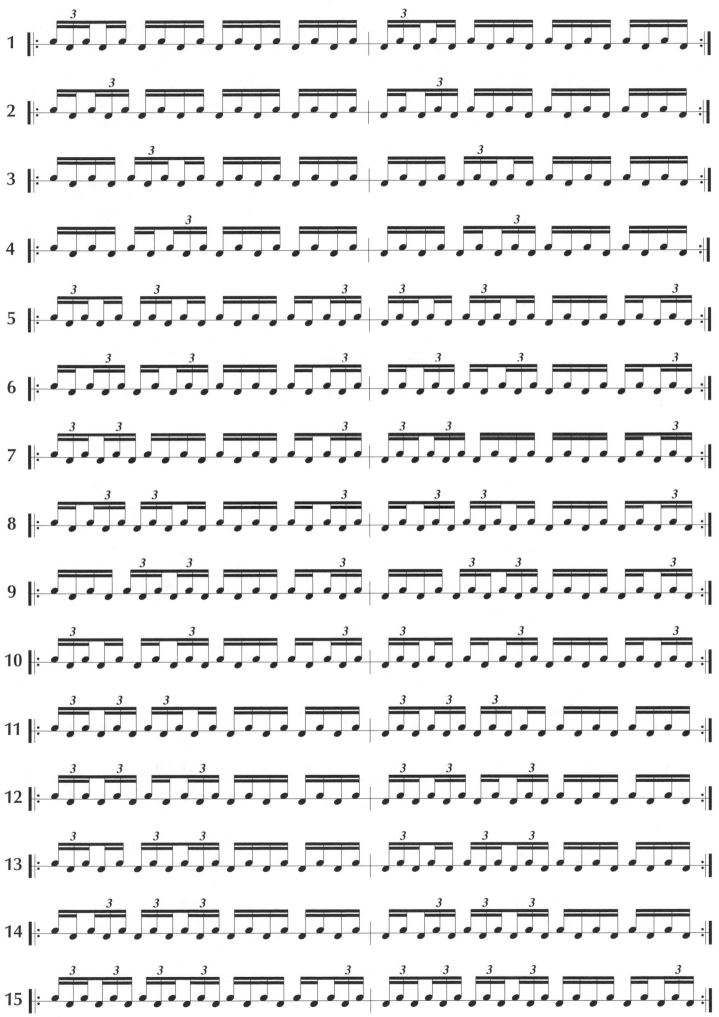

Duple Time 3.2

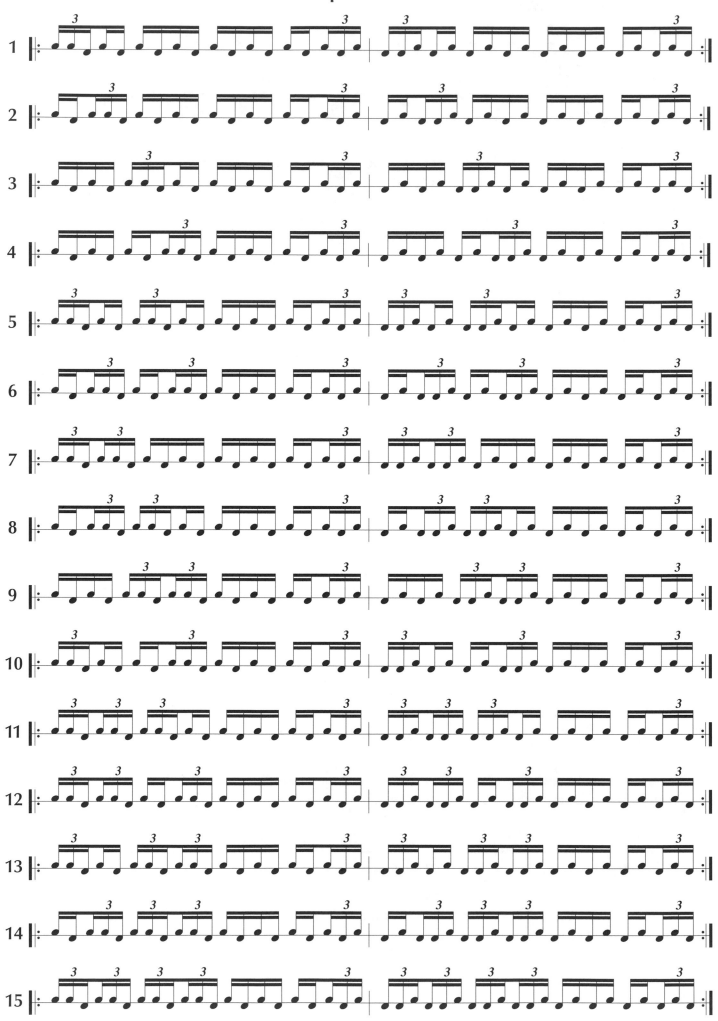

Duple Time 3.3

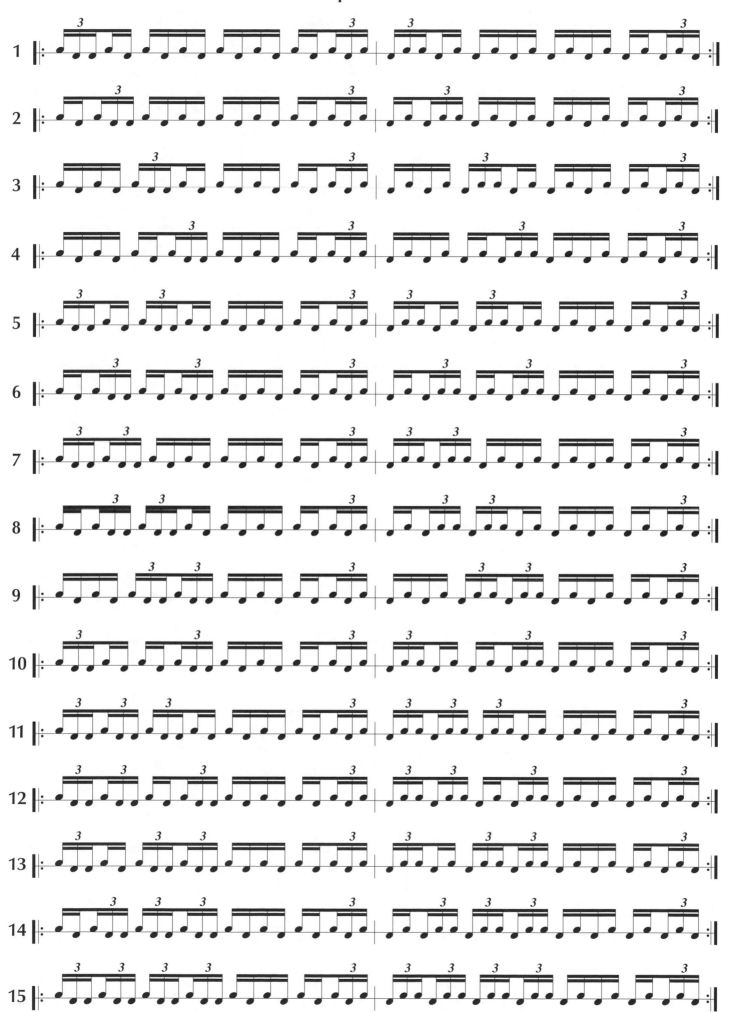

Duple Time 3.4

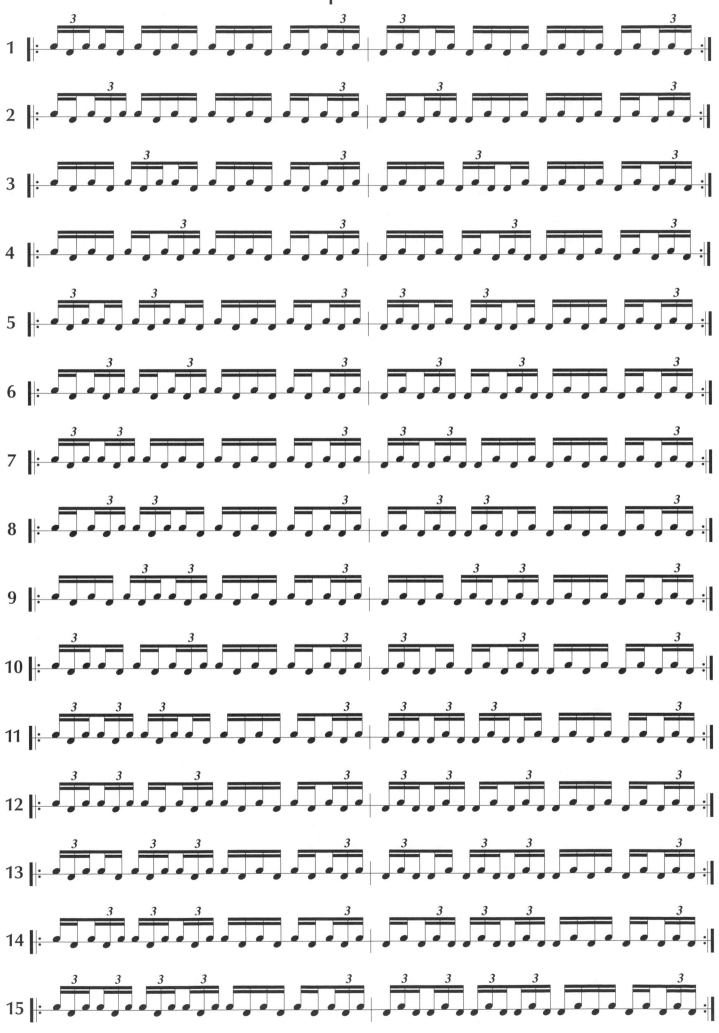

Duple Time 3.5

Duple Time 3.6

Duple Time 3.7

Duple Time 3.8

Duple Time 3.9

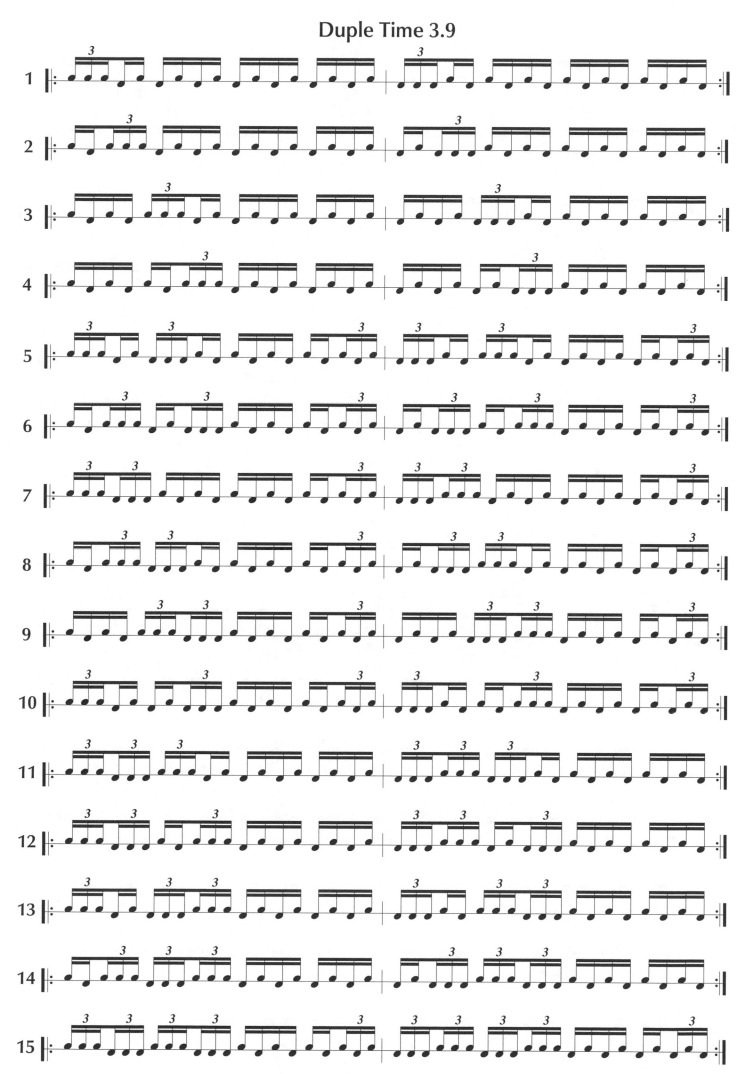

Duple Time 3.10

Groove Melodies 3

Groove Melodies 3

Groove Melodies 3

Groove Melodies 3

Duple Time 4.1

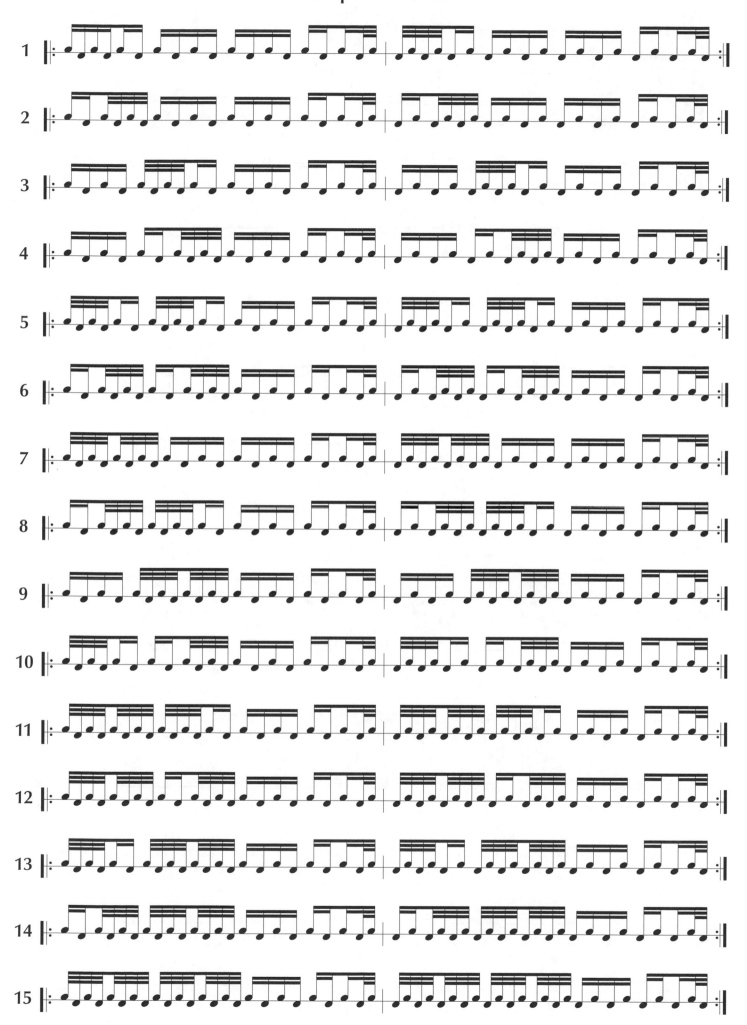

Duple Time 4.2

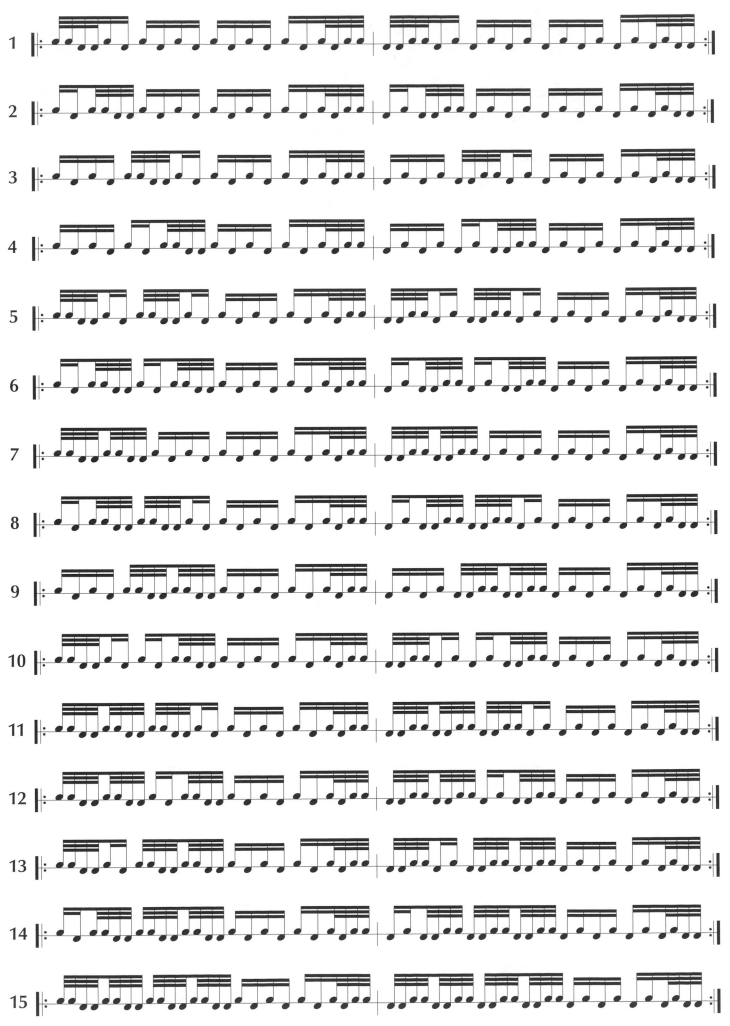

Duple Time 4.3

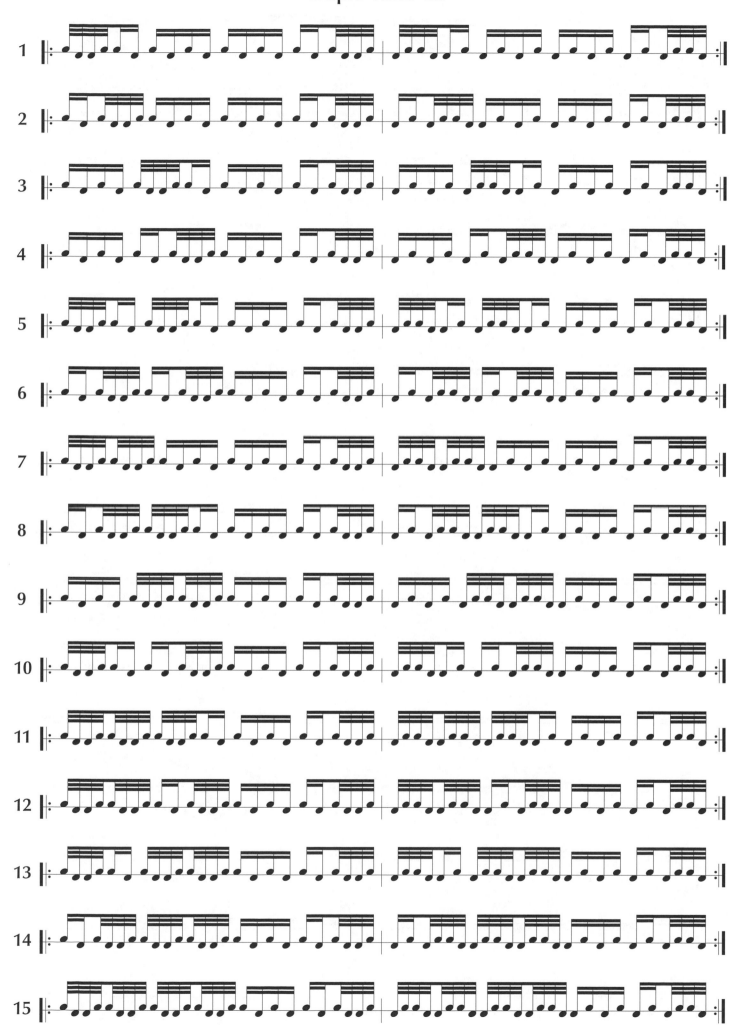

Duple Time 4.4

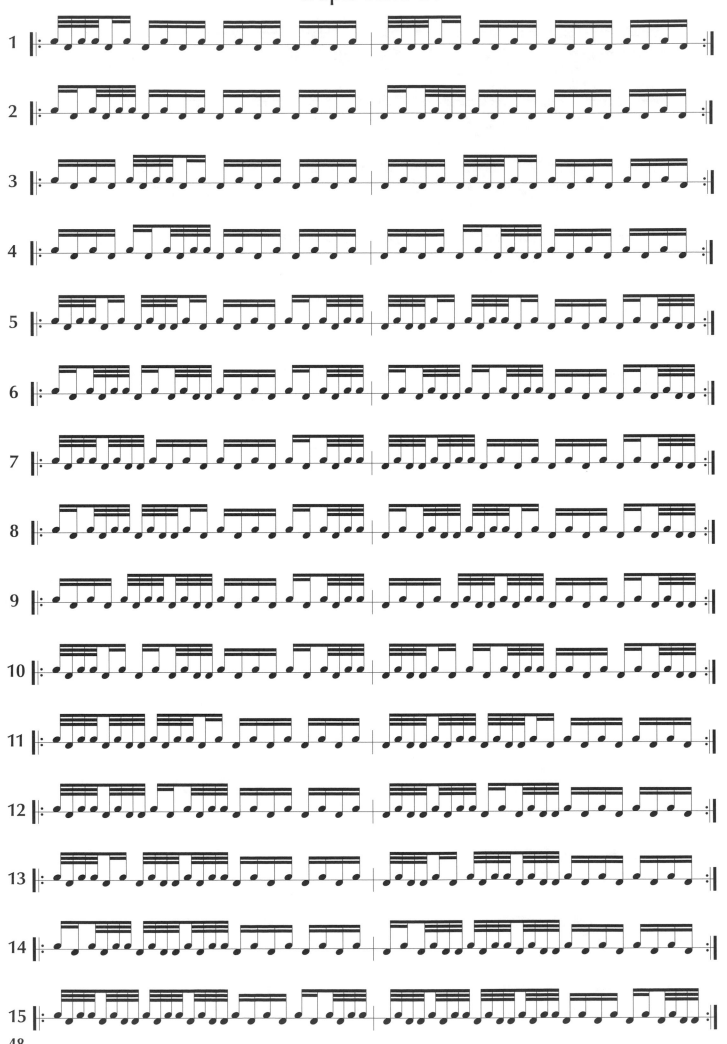

Duple Time 4.5

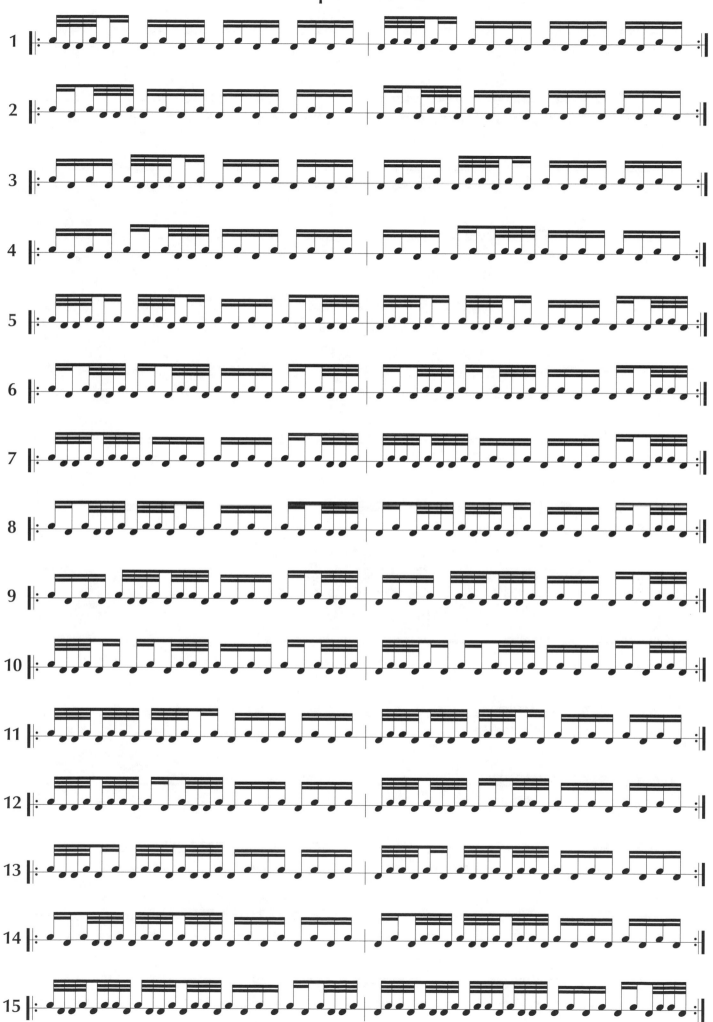

Duple Time 4.6

Duple Time 4.7

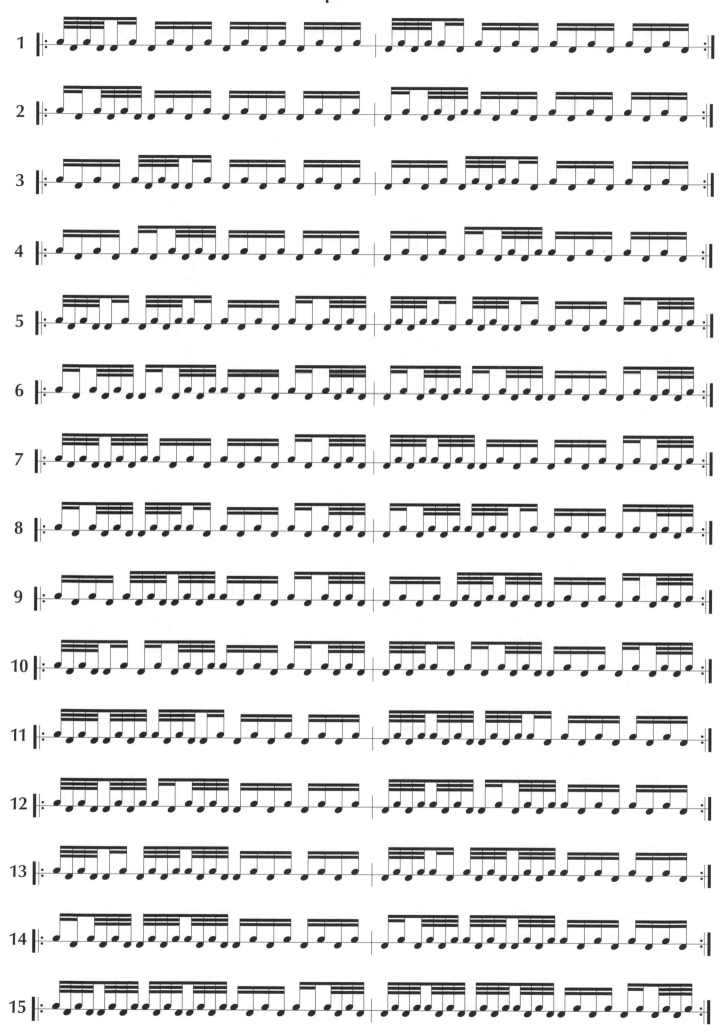

Duple Time 4.8

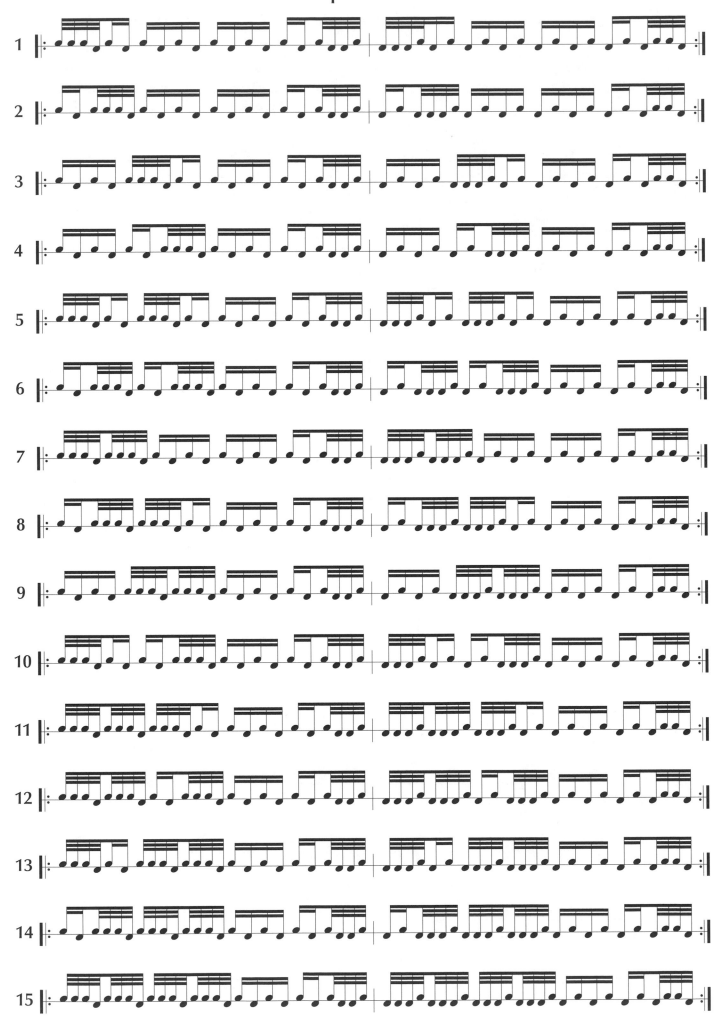

Duple Time 4.9

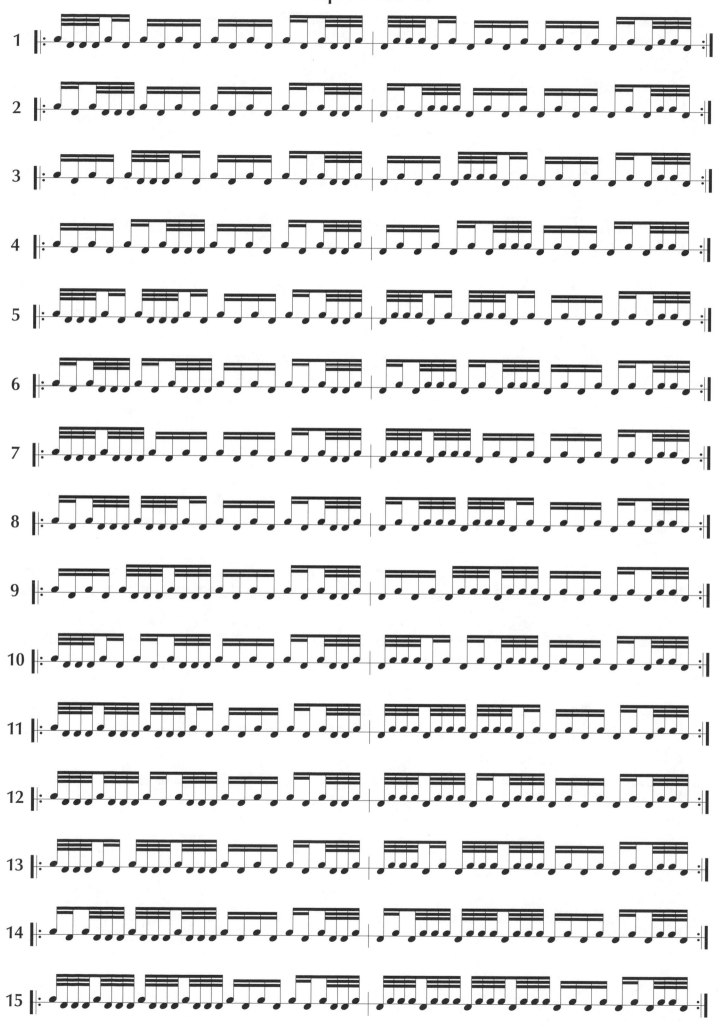

Duple Time 4.10

Groove Melodies 4

Groove Melodies 4

Groove Melodies 4

Groove Melodies 4

PART II

Motion-Balance in Triplet Time

Control Workouts and Groove Melodies
Groups 1–4

Triplet Time 1.1

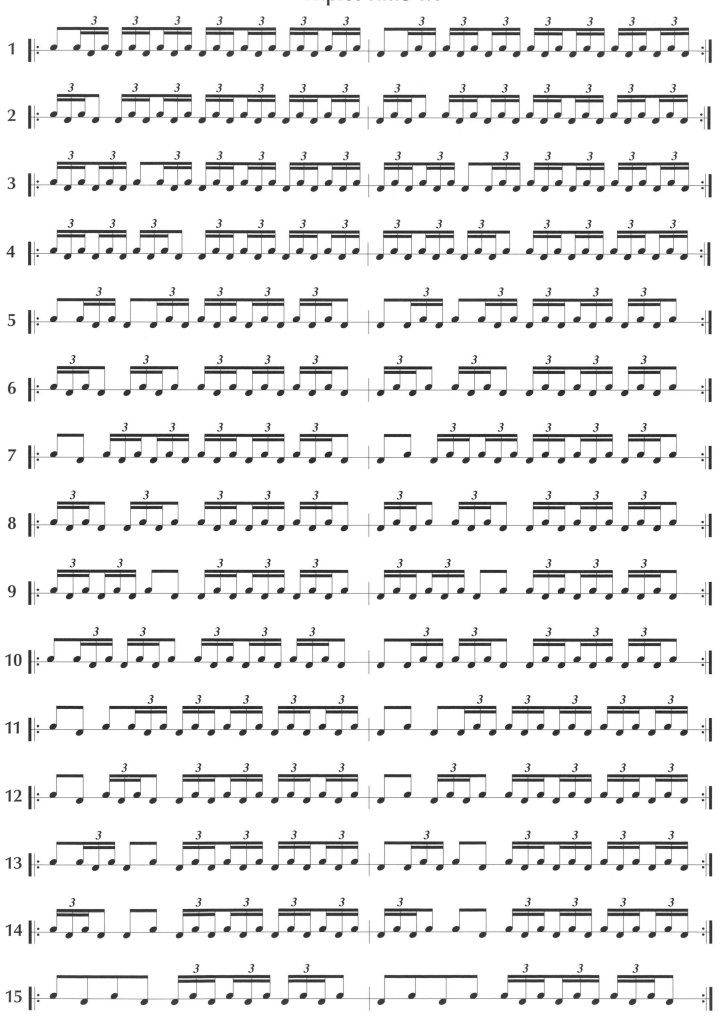

Triplet Time 1.2

Groove Melodies 1

Groove Melodies 1

Triplet Time 2.1

Triplet Time 2.2

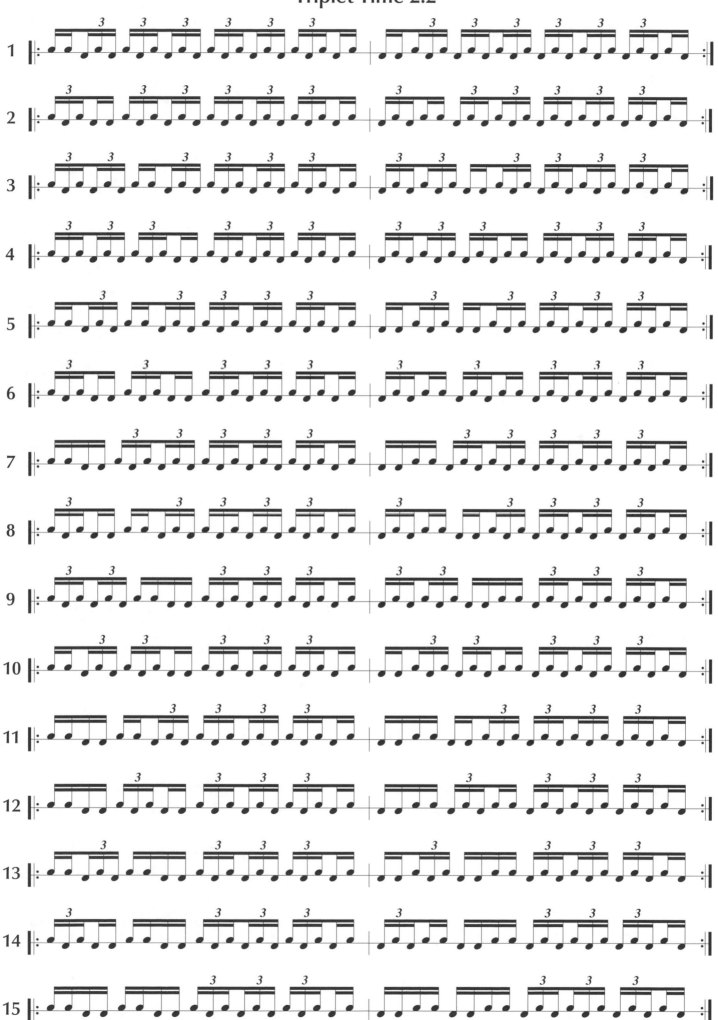

Triplet Time 2.3

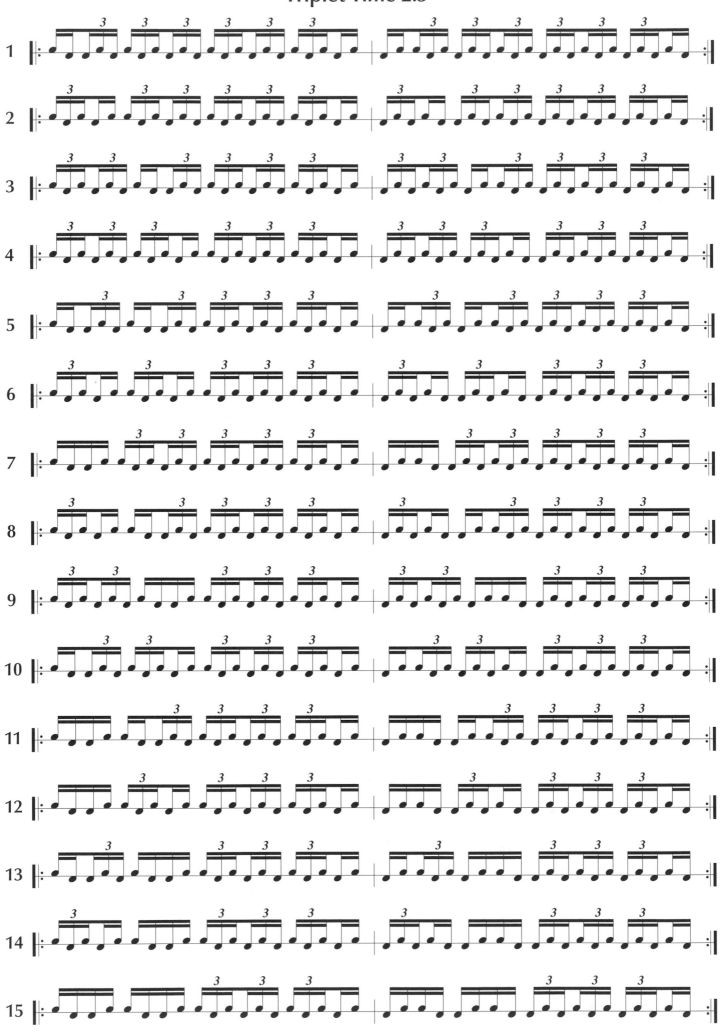

Groove Melodies 2

Groove Melodies 2

Triplet Time 3.1

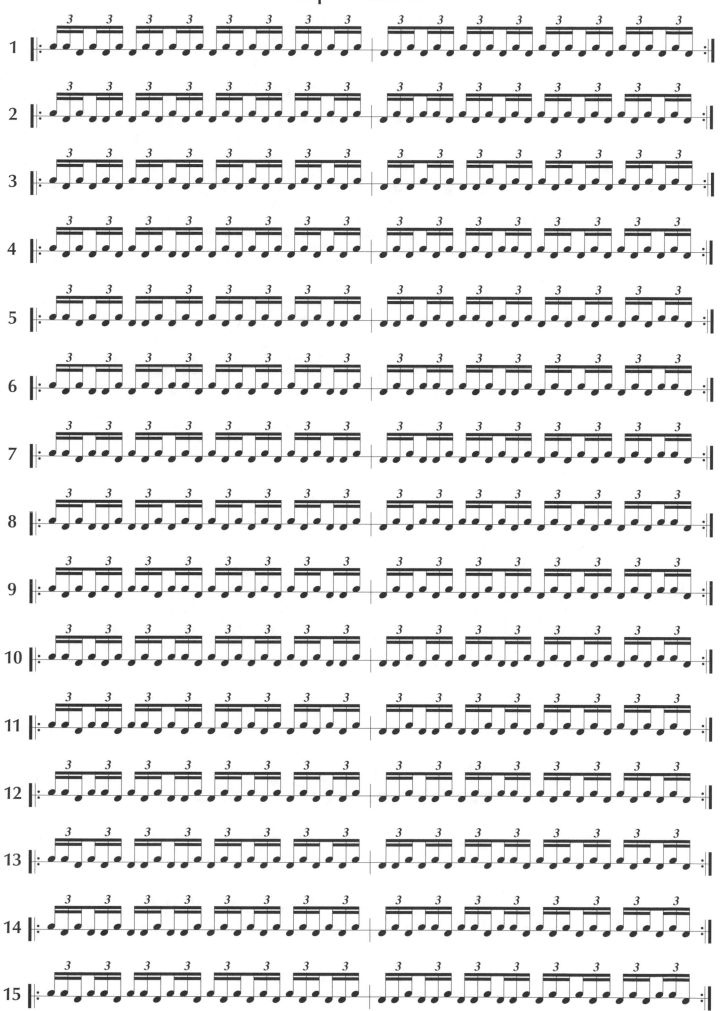

Triplet Time 3.2

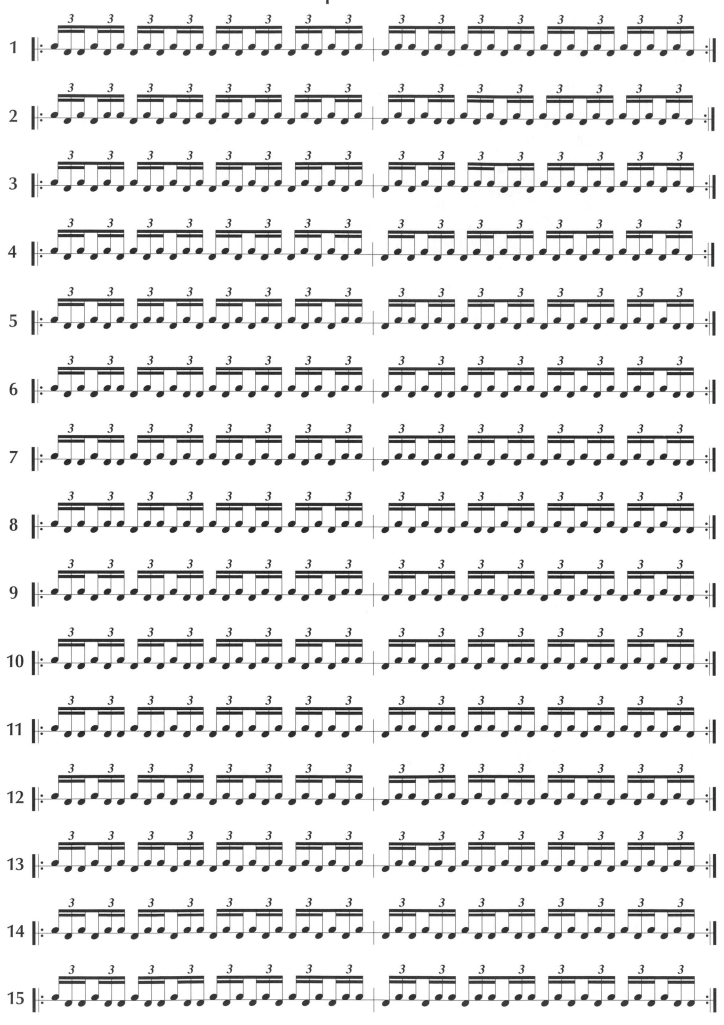

Triplet Time 3.3

Triplet Time 3.4

Triplet Time 3.5

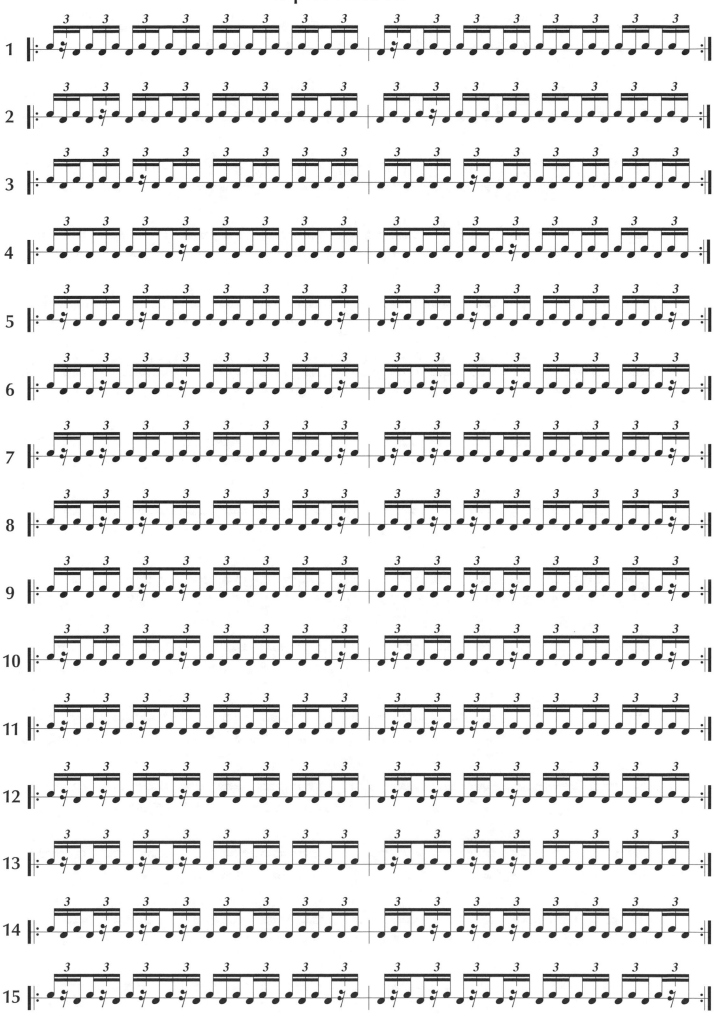

Triplet Time 3.6

Triplet Time 3.7

Triplet Time 3.8

Triplet Time 3.9

Groove Melodies 3

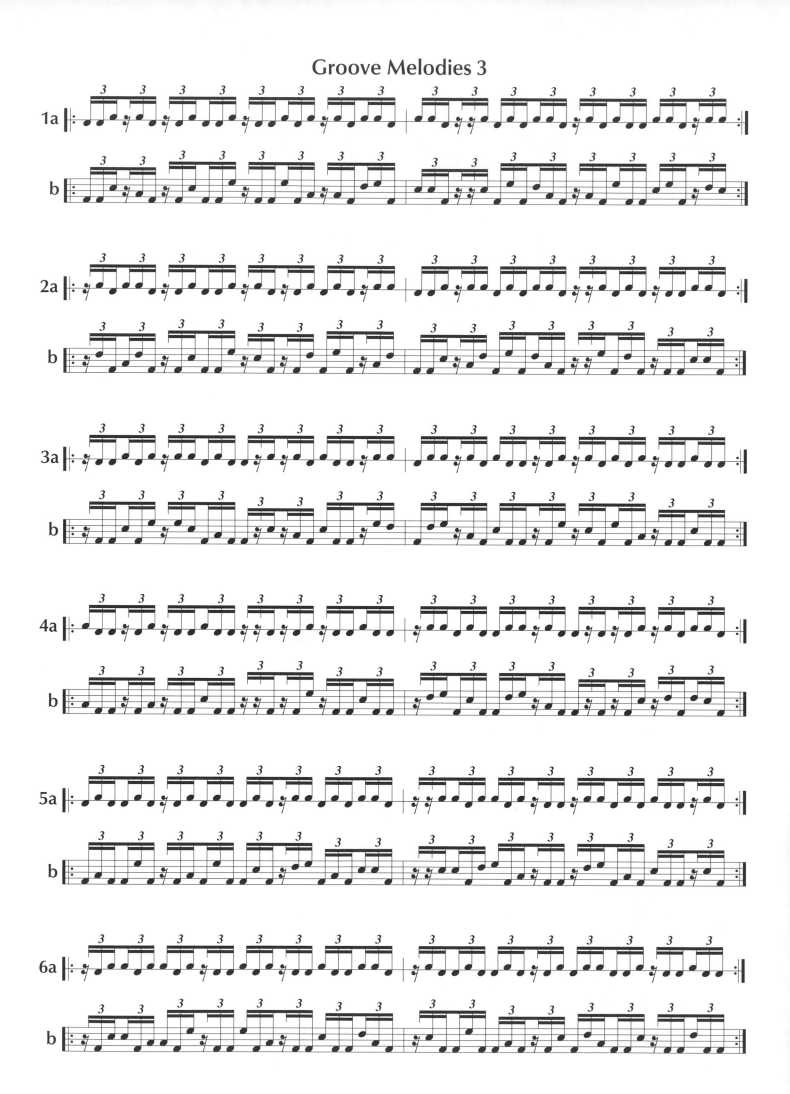

Groove Melodies 3

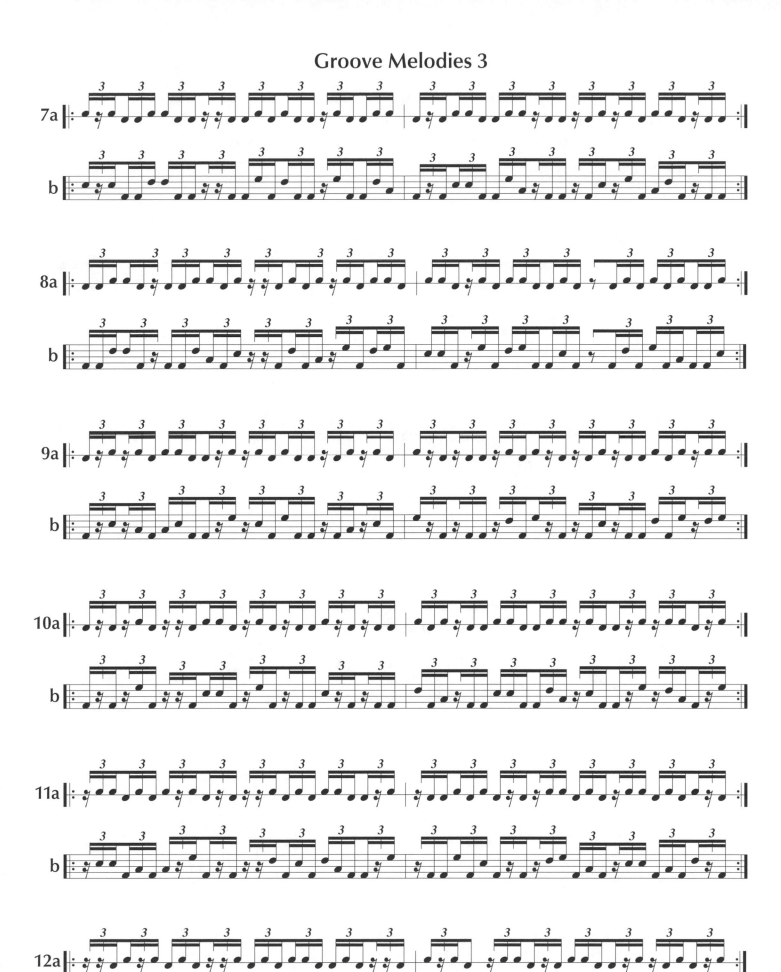

Groove Melodies 3

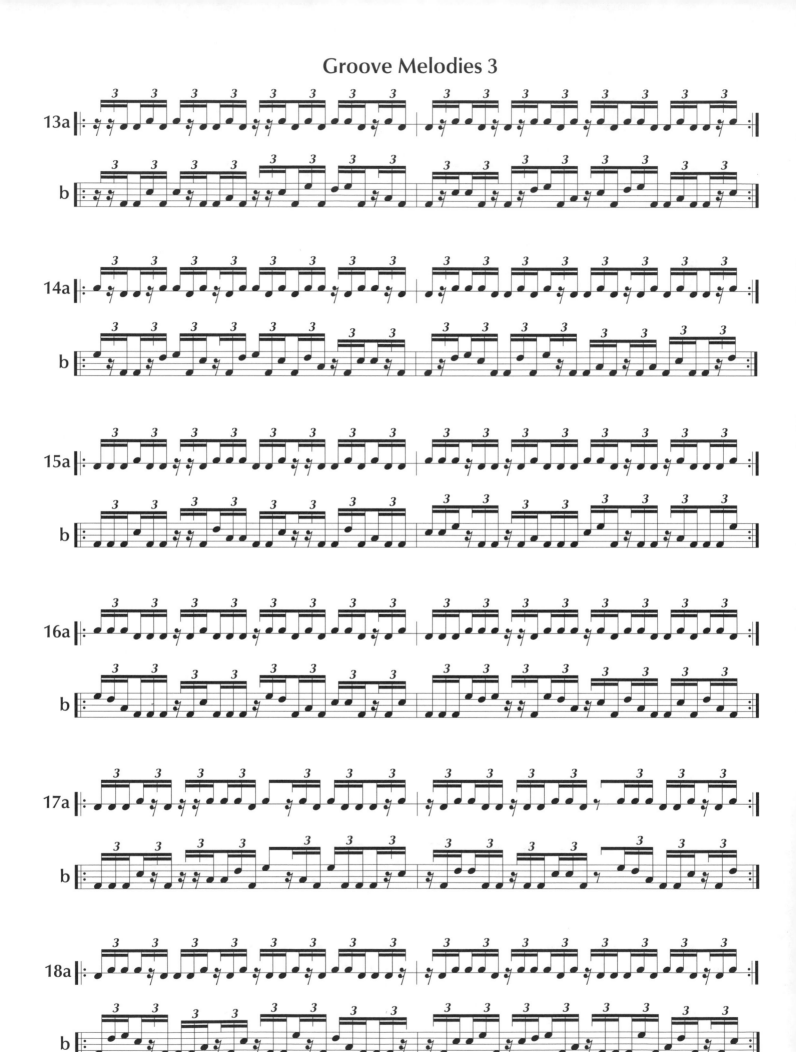

Groove Melodies 3

Triplet Time 4.1

Triplet Time 4.2

Triplet Time 4.3

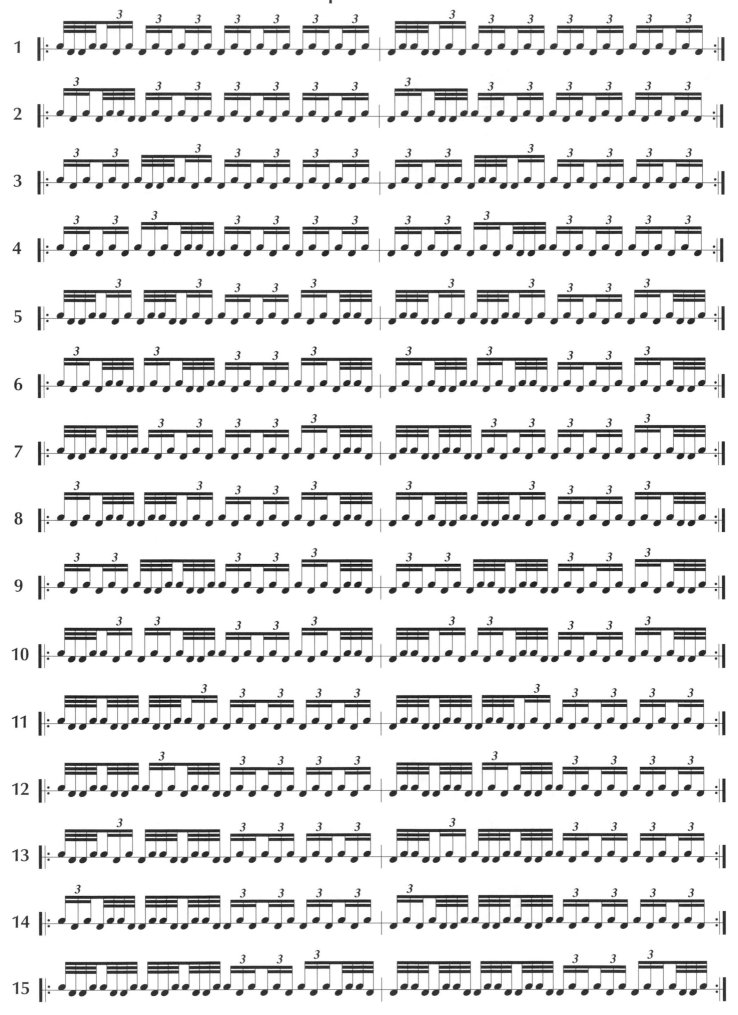

Triplet Time 4.4

Triplet Time 4.5

Triplet Time 4.6

Triplet Time 4.7

Triplet Time 4.8

Triplet Time 4.9

Triplet Time 4.10

Groove Melodies 4

Groove Melodies 4

Groove Melodies 4

Groove Melodies 4

AFTERWORD

By now you're experiencing motion-balance and progressing down the road to interdependence and creative freedom! Progress can be elusive, even difficult, but it also has a shape. We start at the beginning and set out towards mastery. As we improve, we circle back to all the things we thought we learned earlier. Except now we're at a deeper, richer level of experience. We see details we didn't see before.

The most treasured items in my dad's Stone collection are manuscript pages from *Accents & Rebounds*. Stone assigned them to my dad long before his book was published. As a kid, I puzzled over those fragile yellow pages with thick-penciled accents over repeated rhythms. What was being communicated here? Years later, I had the opportunity of a lifetime—I was invited to assist with the new, revised edition of *Accents & Rebounds!*

Pouring over pages of accented studies, I began notating every stroke. We were using a traditional stroke notation system based on arrows. An upward arrow over a note signals an upstroke, a downward arrow is a downstroke and low taps are dashes. It wasn't long before I realized something was wrong. No matter what I did, I couldn't notate the exercise motions correctly.

Over the years, arrow notation had been supplanted by a more cumbersome system using letters. I figured there had to be a 4th stroke symbol that slipped away over the decades. And this missing symbol centered on the full stroke.

I found myself revisiting my dad's collection of Stone notes. I had no idea what I was looking for. I landed on a scrap of paper—in dark pencil a double paradiddle notated with a mark over the first note. I had seen this page many times and thought nothing of it. But years of study and practice had changed me.

The mark was an arrow pointing both up and down—a symbol indicating the down-up motion of a full stroke. Here it was, the missing 4th stroke symbol! After that discovery, we were able to notate all of Stone's accented studies correctly for the new version of *Accents & Rebounds*.

The free stroke, Moeller technique and motion-balance are much more than elements combining into a seamless, total drum technique. They represent an ocean of wisdom we dive ever deeper into. Happy swimming!